THE
SAMOYED
TODAY

RINGPRESS

Published by Ringpress Books Ltd,
PO Box 8, Lydney, Gloucestershire GL15 4YN

Designed by Rob Benson

First Published 2000
© 2000 RINGPRESS BOOKS

ISBN 1 86054 147 X

Printed and bound in Singapore
by Kyodo Printing Co

10 9 8 7 6 5 4 3 2 1

ACKNOWLEDGEMENTS

It would not have been possible for me to write this book without the help of a great many lovers of the breed around the world, and to them I am truly grateful.

I wish to thank the following: Brian Pearson, Janice Brock and Annette Scott, who all contributed to the excellent drawings; Richard M. Venables MRCVS, my vet, for his help in verifying the chapter on health; and, for providing detailed information,

Judi Elford (Canada), Henrik Soeberg (Denmark), Tuula Hamalainen (Finland), Renata Fossati (Italy), Maria Kavcic (Slovenia), Sherry Greener (USA), Bronwyn Hughes, Brian Harries (New Zealand), Irene Rowe (Zimbabwe), and Gerald and Kath Mitchell (UK).

I also wish to thank those who contributed various sections: Gill Austin, Penny Roberts, Ken Warburton, Dave Cox, Pam Landers, Marjorie Steele, Helen Gabb, Annemarie Kolke, Eris Koops, Paul Kabel, Morten Holland, Bjorn Julseth, Carmen Navarro, Marion Wide, Annica Uppstrom and Helen Black.

My thanks to all who contributed to Experts' Choice and to all who sent in some wonderful photographs; sadly, many of these I have been unable to include. In particular I must single out Paulo Delfilippi, who allowed me to raid his entire collection in Italy.

Finally, thanks to Anne Critten, who did all my typing and was patience herself.

All of you have been invaluable.

PAM TAYLOR

Contents

FOREWORD

From my earliest recollection, my family always owned a dog of some sort, mostly of the mixed breed variety, so I was hooked on dogs from the word go. In my very early adult life, I acquired two German Shepherds. I had always admired the Samoyed breed from afar and when my Shepherds eventually passed away, the long arm of coincidence took over.

My work took me into schools and, one day, following a chance conversation with a Primary School Teacher, I learned that her parents owned both a dog and bitch Samoyed. An invitation to visit followed. I found myself enchanted by the breed and my teacher friend was able to put me in touch with Gerard and Kath Mitchell from whom my husband Ray and myself purchased Kiskas Silverstar.

We were then introduced into the world of showing and not long afterwards this bitch was to become Ch. Kiskas Silverstar Of Naduska – our first Samoyed and our first Champion. Silva, as we called her, was subsequently mated to John and Betty James's famous dog Ch. Grenadier Of Crensa. This mating produced a puppy

dog, subsequently bought by the Mitchells, who went on to become Ch. Naduska Grit Of Kiskas.

We kept a litter sister which we mated with Ch. Sammymann White Alpine owned by Catherine Hillier, a dog of marvellous breed type and outstanding coat qualities. This mating produced for us a dog puppy who was to become Ch. Naduska Storm. We then introduced Ch. Hurkur Jingles into our breeding programme and from a mating from his son, Naduska Trailblazer, we obtained Ch. Snowpanda Of Naduska. On yet another of our bitches, we used the very famous Jingles son, Ch. Zamoyski Lucky Star Of Ostiak, the Breed Record-holder. This was to produce another male who became Ch. Naduska Double Oh Seven.

Over the years, we have had our fair share of heartbreak, but we have been able to travel widely, making friends with Samoyed fanciers throughout the world, enjoying with them our common love of this magical breed. It is my hope that by sharing both my knowledge and my experiences, the ultimate beneficiary will be the Samoyed.

1 LIVING WITH SAMOYEDS

Breathtakingly beautiful, the Samoyed is one of the world's most spectacular canines. It is known worldwide as the white dog with the smiling face, who carries the spirit of Christmas in his heart all year round. A true extrovert with a magnetic personality and steady temperament, the Samoyed bestowes the gift of love and happiness to all he meets and greets.

THE SAMOYED ENTHUSIAST

But what exactly is involved when you decide to live with a Samoyed? I asked Dr Ian Murphy, who owns and adores his two Samoyeds and who takes exception to that oft-used phrase "only a pet", to describe what living with Samoyeds means for him. This is what he wrote.

"All the lovely things I expected when first getting my two Samoyeds, a dog and a bitch, came true. Initially, however, I felt that there were two negatives – the daily walk when it was cold, dark and wet, and the daily grooming. These felt like chores. Somewhere in the first year my feelings changed. I learned to put on the radio while grooming and I found slower grooming really focused the task and mind and was much better. When it

is raining heavily, I admit to shortening the walk sometimes, but making a full trip and properly drying out the dogs does make both myself and them feel better – I think!

"Living with them is a joy. Their personalities are different but just seeing them is still a pleasure after many years. To me, daily contacts are a lift and their greetings just a thrill. Initially my dogs used to sleep in a compound, where they still go when no-one is home. Some years ago, I realised that their priority need was the presence of humans, and ever since, I am afraid to say, that they have slept in the bedroom. They do prefer the floor to a dog bed and move around in the night, rather like humans turning over in bed, but they are no trouble at all. In the morning, once we are awake, we receive a friendly, licky greeting to the new day. There have been anxious times when one or other has been ill, but luckily so far, neither has been seriously ill.

"These days I have added to their diet grated vegetables such as carrots, parsnips, cabbage, celery, mangetout, peas and broccoli, cottage and cheddar cheese. Bathing is a big job, but I enjoy doing it and it keeps the dogs looking

Dr Ian Murphy with his Samoyeds in Scotland.

right. Sometimes when I was working all hours, we did use a professional bathing and grooming service. Since I love Scotland as well as the dogs, all four of us go there frequently, camping in remote places. We have an inflatable boat and take both camping kit and the dogs in the boat. The dogs love this and also getting in the tent. They are also keen to get into other people's homes. By this I mean rented cottages and the occasional hotel. The dogs are excellent travellers and have not been known to be car-sick as some breeds are. They have travelled on ferries to the Hebrides, Orkneys and Shetlands without any trouble.

"We even took them on an eight-seater plane flying from Shetland to the Fair Isles. They loved that too, except for the roar of the engines at take-off, which l ed to an initial bit of trembling. The dogs love racing about on the empty beaches and running in the sea. When they were younger, they enjoyed pulling a children's sledge with children on board. I feel their presence has added to many special occasions, but probably the main satisfaction for us is just being together in an ordinary way. They are really good companions. It is hard to think that twelve years ago, I had a short list of breeds. There is only one for me now!"

SAMOYED STORIES
All dog owners think that the breed they have chosen is special – and of course, their own dog is unique! The following stories woud certainly indicate that the Samoyed has a very particular contibution to make as a family companion.

SAVED BY SAMOYEDS
A Samoyed called Samont Gayle, known as Laska, was bred by Thelma and Derek

Pont. From her younger days, Laska had a habit of jumping the garden wall and wandering off. One winter evening in 1981 Laska escaped once again and, wandering in a remote area of moorland, she came across an old man who had collapsed. This gentleman was a Mr Stevenson who earlier in the day had set out for a walk. Laska had the presence of mind to curl up beside the old man, thus keeping him warm with her body heat. The next morning, the two of them were so found. In recognition of Laska's achievement, she was presented with a prestigious award. This was the Pro-dogs Gold Lifesaving award and she was further honoured with a decorated scroll, presented to her owners at a dinner, by the Northern Samoyed Society.

In 1982, 67 year-old William Diddridge was working as a part-time Security Officer two nights a week at a petrol depot on the mouth of a river two miles away from the nearest habitation. His five-and-a-half year old Samoyed bitch, Nikki, whose real name was Sibersam Silver Bubbles, accompanied her master in his job. One morning, at 5am as the night shift finished, Mr Diddridge found that his car in the car park was completely covered with snow. Fastening a rope to the end of Nikki's lead he set off for home which was four miles away. The first two hundred yards involved a walk alongside the sea shore. Since the tide was high, the spray froze on both man and dog. Mr Diddridge found that he could not remove his spectacles since they were frozen to his hair.

Nikki's coat was spiked with ice and covered with heavy snow, and after travelling two miles, she was twice her normal size. The pair ploughed through six-foot snowdrifts, Nikki pulling and tugging all the time, refusing to allow her master to stop and rest. Eventually both reached the main road and finally arrived home, frozen stiff, the journey having taken almost four hours. Nikki was wrapped in blankets on her arrival home. Her feet were covered in ice and were the size of saucers. Mr Diddridge claimed his dog had undoubtedly saved his life.

An elderly lady once saw me out with two of my Samoyeds and her face lit up as she hurried over to talk to me. She told me that her maiden name was Alice Ward and that when she was a little girl of three years of age, her life was saved by a Samoyed. It seems the mother of this lady was a housekeeper for a well-to-do gentleman who owned a large house in North London. One day, the mother working at the top of the house with her husband, who also worked there, heard the frantic barking of Peter, a Samoyed dog, belonging to the owner who was away. All of a sudden the frantic barking ceased.

The couple deliberated whether they should investigate, hesitated and then went down into the garden. They then saw their little daughter, Alice. She had fallen headlong into the lily pond. The dog, Peter, seeing what had happened, seized the little girl by the velvet collar of her dress and dragged her head clear of the water. He was still holding the collar when her parents arrived, hence the silence after the barking. After all the ensuing years, Alice told me that she could remember the incident vividly. It was a sunny day and she had seen water beetles crawling on the lily leaves. She bent down for a closer look and toppled in. What presence of mind the dog Peter had and what a happy ending!

9

Pat Hemmings once owned a dog called Baron Tobias. One night when she was in bed with an electric blanket, it started to smoulder. Pat had taken some tablets to combat flu and was in a deep sleep. She awoke to find the dog pulling her out of bed by her wrist and the room full of smoke. She bears the marks on her wrist today but acknowledges that she probably would not be alive now if it was not for her plucky Baron Tobias.

SAMOYED SURVIVORS
Samzak Ice Bear, known as Storm, lived by the seaside with his owners Jill and Carl Lord, and Storm was used to being taken for his daily exercise along the beach. One day in 1987, Storm got out and took himself for a walk along the beach heading north. What Storm did not realise was that the sea comes in very quickly in that area and very soon he became surrounded by water and had to swim for it. Luckily for the dog, before he became too exhausted, he was spotted by an electrician who was driving his van slowly along the Promenade in this more isolated part. Coincidentally, this gentleman also owned a Samoyed dog. Wading into the sea, the rescuer was able to reach Storm and, as he was wearing his name disc, returned him wet, dripping but alive to the Lords. It must have been Storm's lucky day.

In 1979, two-year-old Ky, which is Cornish for dog, went missing from his home. His owners thought he had been stolen. They advertised in local and national newspapers and made about a hundred telephone calls in an attempt to trace the dog. One month later a fisherman setting lobster pots in the sea spotted Ky on a ledge which was invisible from the cliff top.

The coastguard and police were alerted and Ky was hauled to safety in a sacking sling. His owners were delirious with delight when Ky was returned to them. He was dirty and thin and appeared to have lost half his body weight, but there were no injuries. It was thought that Ky had fallen into a shaft, bouncing against the wall, into water at the bottom, which broke his fall. From there he must have scrambled out onto the ledge.

The remarkably dense double coat of the Samoyed gives protection in freezing conditions.

THE SYMPATHETIC SAMOYED

Frank Maxwell worked until his retirement as a group worker and counsellor at a Day Centre for those suffering with problems of the mind – depression, phobias, intense loneliness, lack of self-esteem etc. He attended twice a week taking with him Karaholme Sarah, who was a Samoyed bitch with a disposition described as sweet and affectionate. From the outset, Sarah's visits were an enormous success, proving to be of great therapeutic value. She appeared to have an instinct to seek out those members who were most in need of overt demonstrations of affection. She would walk up to their side, squat herself down or snuggle between their legs to demand affection. The immediate effect was seen in a softening of their facial expressions as they realised that here was a creature which made no difficult or heavy demands but freely gave of love. Thus the tension and sadness were seen to melt away. Should Sarah fail to come to Sandfield House for any reason she would be missed by all.

SAMOYEDS AND CHILDREN

Eleven-year-old Kerry Halpin was born deaf. When she was ten, she had completed intensive treatment for life-threatening cancer, following the discovery of a tumour next to her kidneys.

On her recovery, she was given a gift from a nearby animal sanctuary she frequently visited. The gift was a two-year-old Samoyed bitch called Fox who was blind. Between the two of them a huge bond then formed. Kerry would look out for Fox and Fox would become Kerry's ears. Since deaf children are difficult to rouse in the morning, Fox

Special relationships often develop between Samoyeds and children – as long as both learn to respect each other.

would hassle Kerry until she awoke. In April 1999, Kerry and Fox won the WAG (Willing and Giving) Child Companion/Animal Award.

Since Samoyeds are a kind breed of dog, they are marvellous with children and just love being with them. Although they can stand a fair amount of pummelling, children should be trained to respect them. It is also reassuring to know that they are completely trustworthy with children of all ages. If there are other family pets, after an initial few days getting to know one another, it would be quite usual for them to become firm friends.

THE GUARDING SAMOYED

The home of Brenda Walker was burgled one day during the afternoon. She suspected that the dogs might have let

Samoyeds love to be part of the action— this trio were guest attendants at an Australian wedding.

the burglars in. The offenders were eventually caught and questioned. They spoke about the 'beautiful white dogs' and said that they actually played with them!

The Samoyed is certainly not a guard dog. Many are even great friends with the postman. They have a great need to be raised as part of the family rather than being stuck in a kennel. This is because, in their origins, they lived as family with the Samoyed people, only being used by them for herding the reindeer. However, they do have a sense of danger and will warn by barking.

THE HERDING SAMOYED

Many years ago, while I was exercising one of my Samoyeds off the lead on some land belonging to a wealthy country landowner, the dog disappeared over the brow of a hill. On surmounting the hill myself, I came across an amazing sight. Formed into a tight circle was a group of about forty prize racehorses including polo ponies and hunters. They had been herded this way by my very excited Samoyed who was dashing around them yapping with delight. It was obviously the completely natural herding instinct taking over.

THE SHOW-OFFS

When Muriel Hopkin had her first Samoyed dog, Scaf, she attended a Club Championship Show held in a picture gallery. There were pillars everywhere which considerably hampered the judging. Miss Keyte-Perry was the judge and, because she could not bend very far, a long stool with a basket-work top was brought into the ring for the dogs to stand on. Mrs Hopkin claims Scaf was a naughty dog and when it came to her turn to move him, from behind a pillar, he took off, feet hardly touching the ground, and the stool, three chairs and the steward were sent flying!

The White Fluff Club of Holland was formed by Sonja Hozeman and other assistants in the Netherlands. A team of twelve well-trained Samoyeds, together with their handlers, wearing matching track suits with a White Fluff logo, go through an impressive routine, performed in front of a live audience with Sonja blowing a whistle to synchronize events. Following the obedience demonstration, the ring is quickly cleared and a twenty-item Agility course quickly assembled. It is a competent display and every credit must be given to both the organisers and the participants, especially the dogs.

It would seem that Samoyeds are currently being very successfully used in the marketing field. No-one would doubt their appeal. Samoyeds have been used in TV advertising for Coca Cola, Hoover and for Tesco. In the 1980s, there was a Samoyed by the name of Tundra who was very hot property in Hollywood. She was a considerable earner for her owners, appearing in numerous advertisements as well as TV's *Love Boat* and the film *Against all Odds*. In 1983, she won the Patsy award, which is the animal equivalent of the Oscar.

From the end of November 1988 to the end of January 1989, a team of sixteen Samoyeds took it in turns to take part in the pantomime, Snow White and the Seven Dwarfs. Two dogs at a time were required for an ice scene, where Snow White lay poisoned on a sleigh, drawn by the dogs and handled by Cossacks. Since the production sometimes entailed three performances a day, I drew up a rota of enthusiasts and their dogs, who were required to report to the Green Room prior to their performance on stage. It goes without saying that the dogs loved every minute of it and would go wild with delight when they were driven to the theatre. Typical show-offs! Of course the children in the audience adored them and there were many "Oohs and Aahs".

WINDSURFING
Some years ago, Mr and Mrs Stoute of Rotterdam, Holland came over to the

Stars of the stage – an unusual production of 'Snow White and the Seven Dwarfs'.

The aquatic Samoyed: Naduska Hussar has taken to both windsurfing and swimming.

UK and bought a male Samoyed from us. He was Naduska Hussar and was known in Holland as Akka. A couple of years later, we received from the Stoutes a photograph showing their daughter windsurfing together with Akka. Apparently, he took to this sport like a duck to water and also enjoyed swimming. Akka's brother, Seeker, who we kept, also loved the water, swimming round the local pond at every opportunity. I am also aware that there are windsurfing Samoyeds in Canada, having seen a photograph of one windsurfing with its owner on Green Lake.

GETTING IN A SPIN
Having established that the Samoyed carries a superbly dense double coat, we come to yet another aspect of keeping these wonderful dogs as pets. The coat provides excellent material for spinning into yarn.

Care should be taken when grooming and the combings put into suitable piles. All the short hair from the legs and head should be discarded, along with the coarse hair from the tail, trousers and outer guard hairs. The soft undercoat from the first few days of moulting, provides the best quality fibres to make finer garments worn nearer the skin. Combing from any subsequent grooming may be a little coarser and therefore suitable for outer-wear garments such as jackets and coats. It is essential to keep the combings in paper not plastic bags, since if the wool is cut off from air it will go yellow.

Providing the dogs are kept clean, it is not necessary to wash the combings at this stage or indeed card them and they can be 'spun in the grease', that is unwashed, making it easier to handle. The technique for spinning dog combings is a little different to that of sheep's fleece. The latter is easier to spin due to the tiny 'hooks' on the hairs which hold the fibres together and therefore it requires less of a twist. Dog hair is smoother and needs more twist or it will fall apart.

It is helpful to decide what you want to knit before spinning the yarn to enable you to achieve the thickness you require for the garment. There are many ways of altering the effect of the finished yarn, such as mixing Samoyed wool with sheep fleece or plying (twisting together) 1 ply of Samoyed yarn with 1 ply of a commercial silk yarn of a different colour for a beautiful subtle shade, thereby doing away with the lengthy business of dying the finished yarn.

Once spun and plied, the yarn is made into hanks. Equipment for this job is available but I find winding the yarn around a tea-tray and tying the strands together at intervals is an effective way. The hanks are then washed in hot water using washing-up liquid to take out the grease. Do not squeeze or agitate too much at this stage or the yarn will begin to "felt" or fall apart. Rinse in cold water to try to shrink it, as it is far better to shrink it at this stage than when the garment is completed. Having produced sufficient yarn for your intended garment it is wise to use an open or lacy pattern to allow air to flow through, as Samoyed yarn is very warm to wear.

To conclude on a humorous note: I was once approached by two elderly gentlemen from Wales who had heard I spun Samoyed wool. After a lengthy telephone conversation a day was

arranged when they would bring three bin bags of combings for spinning. However, it ultimately transpired their last Samoyed dog had died 10 years earlier and the bags had been stored in a shed. You can imagine my horror when I opened up the bags only to find them alive with almost every conceivable creepy-crawly imaginable. It was a case of getting them out of my lounge and onto the bonfire post-haste.

On another occasion while doing a craft fair, and displaying some garments alongside some photographs of the dogs who supplied the yarn, I was set upon by a young teenage girl who thought I had killed the dogs to obtain the fabric! As

Gill Austin at her spinning wheel, wearing a homespun Samoyed jacket.

you can see, spinning can be absorbingly happy, and it can produce some humorous moments. Articles made from Samoyed yarn will not shrink in washing because it is not a crimped fibre like wool. A spinning wheel can normally be purchased when visiting a craft fair. A local library should also be able to supply details of any local spinning organisations.

SURFING WITH YOUR SAM

More and more of us now have access to personal computers and the growth of popularity of the Internet and the World Wide Web has been phenomenal. For many, the first steps towards 'going global' may seem technical and confusing. What can we get from this resource? How do you find your way around the bewildering world of web sites and e-mail? More importantly, what benefit will the Samoyed owner get from the Net? The first thing to remember is that it can be easy – and that help is usually at hand. Fear should not hold you back.

What do you need to start? A computer, a modem, some software and access to a telephone line. Most modern computers come complete with their own modem (a modem is the piece of equipment that lets your computer 'talk' through the phone line). Alternatively you can buy an external modem – a small box that plugs into your computer. The software is what links you to the 'service provider' – the company that routes your mail to you and provides you with access to the Internet. Today companies are falling over themselves to give you this software for free. All you have to do is decide which one you want. So, your modem is sorted, you have installed your

software; your provider has given you your e-mail address and password; you have introduced yourself to the 'helpline' (hello, I'm new at all this, and my computer says that I have got it wrong....); and you are ready to 'surf'. But where do you want to go?

SAMFANS

One of the first places you can visit is Samfans on www.samfans.org – a website run by Samoyed owners for Samoyed owners. From the Samfans 'homepage' you will be able to look at pictures of members' Samoyeds on the Refrigerator Door – this is a collection of photographs, regularly updated, sent in by Samfans. Here you will also find out

The World Wide Web gives Samoyed enthusiasts access to valuable breed information.

how to join the Samfans e-mail group – some 500 Samoyed fans across the world who share information, advice, and stories about that one abiding interest! The group 'discusses' lots of different topics – from rescues to remedies, exercise regimes to local show results, as well as gentle tales of Samoyed behaviour. Sometimes the debates can become heated, with responses coming in from all over the world. If your Sam does well at a show, you might want to tell the list; you will receive warm congratulations from around the globe! Be warned, Samfans is a busy e-mail group and you can find yourself receiving up to 100 e-mails a day.

From the Samfans site you will also be able to 'link' to other, mainly US Samoyed sites such as the Samoyed Club of America and, from there, to a wide range of sites across the world. When last checked there were links to the American Kennel Club; e-mail addresses for clubs across Australia; and sites in New Zealand, Canada, Denmark (the magnificently named Samojedhundeklubben i Danmark), Finsams in Finland, Sweden, the Netherlands, Ireland and Italy. In addition there are also a host of individuals' 'home' pages – Sammy owners who have put together their own sites on the web – with news and pictures of their dogs. There is not, as yet, a group for primarily UK Samoyed enthusiasts – but with more and more people going on-line every day, it will not be long before one of the more computer literate surfers gathers together a group – 'BritSams' perhaps?

OTHER SITES
More generally are the sites that are run by the Kennel Club, or the dog papers' sites – which include news round-ups and breeder information. There are also canine shopping centres – one-stop shops for all your doggy needs, and lots of companies now have e-mail or web addresses on their advertisements. You may find that you want to buy from the Internet, and it is as well to remember that you should take care to order from reputable companies, just as you would with mail order shopping. If you do not feel comfortable sending your credit card details over the Net then you can get the product details and order by phone or mail. Here again you will find that many sites have links to others, and part of the fun is to see where you end up! If you like a site and want to be able to visit again in the future, save the address in your 'favourites' file and you will be able to go straight to it the next time.

Increasingly, some of the larger Championship shows are becoming 'wired' and it is now possible to make your entries to one or two shows over the Net. It will not be long before more societies offer this service. Fosse Data, the specialist catalogue printing company, runs a results service for the general Championship shows, so you can find out who won what.

The Internet is a quick and cheap way to research a wide variety of topics and a very useful forum for the exchange of information and it can be a great way to make new friends. Take the plunge and try it out, but remember that your correspondence on the Net will be seen by a lot of people – after all, you can be in touch with the other side of the world in the time it takes to press the 'send' button.

2 ORIGINS OF THE BREED

The breed takes its name from a group of nomadic people, of Finnic origin, collectively known as the Samoyeds. These tribespeople lived in Northern Russia, in the land which lay between the White Sea and Yenesei in Western Siberia, and in the regions including Kanin, Petchora and the Islands of Nova Zembla and Wagai Kalgnev. These were people of Mongolian stock joining the Laps who lived in these regions from prehistoric times.

THE SAMOYED PEOPLE

On the basis of language, the Samoyed people could be divided into three great races: Yurak Samoyeds, Tawgi Samoyeds and Ostiak Samoyeds, with this last group sub-dividing again into two smaller tribes, the Yenesei and the Kamassinzi. It is thought that there were originally nine clans, or tribes, of Samoyed people. Only four groups are in existence today – the Nenets, Nganasans, Selkups and Enets. The Samoyed people were of Mongolian appearance. They were known to be very sociable, delighting in gossip, with their smiles almost continuous. They were small; males averaging 5' 5" and women averaging 4' 11" in height. The whiteness of their teeth were attributed to a fondness for chewing the resin of the red pine. The men were known to be inveterate snuff-takers.

The spelling of the name Samoyed is various. Samoied, Samoyad, Samoyade and Samoyed were all used at the turn of the twentieth century. It was F.G.

A Nenet tribesman.

The lifestyle of the present-day Nenet tribesman has scarcely changed; they still rely on their chooms as a principal means of accommodation.

Jackson, the great explorer, who claimed that the word should be pronounced Sam-o-yed – and so quickly that the 'o' was slurred.

He stated that the phonetic form could be Sammyad. Yuraks pronounced the name Samo-yad or even Sam-yad. Today, we opt for the easier Samoyed – or just plain Sam. Although the Samoyeds referred to themselves as Hasavo, which is equivalent to 'men', the name Samoyed in Russian translates to 'self-eater' and to us that would mean cannibal. In a way, this is probably a quirk of translation. Much later, the Samoyed people were to become so resentful of it, that they presented a petition to Stalin to have this changed. This met with the right response and it is now widely accepted that this name now means 'self-feeder', or 'provider'. The tribe people lived in tents known as chooms. They had both a summer and a winter choom.

Basically, these were made using twenty or so poles of some twenty feet in length. The winter choom would be covered with reindeer skins and the inside covered with furs. It was impervious to snow and wind and could be made really hot with the fire in the centre. Reindeer skins would also serve as bed blankets. A summer choom would

be made of bright amber sheets of finely prepared bark, each seamed and sewn with sinew thread. The floor would be soft, covered by thick, dry moss. Over the fire in the middle was hung a kettle and pot, hung from a wooden hook, suspended from two sticks, fixed across the choom and lashed at the end to the choom poles. Above was an opening of some 30" to 2' between the top of the choom poles.

The Samoyeds loved tea, which they would drink seasoned with reindeer milk. They also loved the luxury of toast which they made by spreading a lump of rye-dough on two or three sticks and holding it in the fire. Sometimes the only piece of furniture in a choom would be a chest, which would hold the treasured possessions of three or four china cups and saucers.

The men would wear what is known as a militza, made from reindeer skins, and long boots made out of sealskin, known as pimmies. They would carry a long pole, termed a harray, for driving reindeer. A piece of iron was attached to the end which would be used for testing the ice when crossing rivers. Bows and arrows would also be used for hunting foxes, bears, seals and walrus.

The Samoyed women invariably wore a pigtail under a tight-fitting cap, which they decorated with metal ornaments. The wives (babba) frequently rowed boats and put up the chooms. The children would dress as miniature reproductions of their parents, playing with bows and arrows and, sometimes, a model of a reindeer sledge.

THE REINDEER HERDS

Almost the sole interest of the Samoyeds was their reindeer, and their only exercise was in rounding them up. The reindeer were much prized for food, clothing, milk and transport. In fact, the reindeer were the equivalent of the camels of the desert. They fed on lichens, moss and grasses of the tundra. When the ground was covered with snow, the reindeer would paw this away to get to the food.

The Samoyeds would annually migrate south to avoid the wild winter weather, collecting any wood they could find, since it was scarce. When seeking a site for the winter camp, they would look for an abundance of iceland moss and wildfowl. The winter tent was left in the spot for two weeks, sometimes more. The herders made the rounds of the herd each day, covering a huge circle in the process. When the moss was eaten up they would move to another spot, but the choom was left at the former site and only moved when the new tundra was too far away.

A great disaster was deep snow, forming an ice crust, preventing the reindeer digging down to the moss. Certain Samoyedic groups harnessed their reindeer for carrying packs. This usually occurred with the southern groups and was the forerunner to the sleigh. On Nova Zembla and Wagai, dogs were used to harness the sledges, between three and twelve being used. In 1997 the *Daily Express* ran a centre-page spread on the Nenet tribe, when a summer tribe was discovered at Amderma on the Kara Sea. This caused great excitement among anthropologists because of their rarity, and they were described as 'the tribe that time forgot'.

THE SAMOYED DOGS

The dogs of the Samoyed people lived closely with them, wandering the Tundra and being allowed to sleep in the chooms when they had puppies or in the very bad weather when the temperature would dip 50°C or more below freezing. For the rest of the time, the dogs would dig deep holes in the ground and nestle in, with only their black noses peeking forth.

There was an intensely close relationship between the tribespeople and their dogs. Although living conditions were incredibly hard, the dogs were viewed and appreciated as personal

The reindeer, herded together near the summer camp at Amderma on the Kara sea.

family belongings. They were used to herd the reindeer, in much the same way as a sheepdog would herd sheep. They were used to pull canoes along the rivers as well as pulling the sledges. They seemed greatly to enjoy taking part in hunting bear or walrus, bravely encountering some ferocious attacks. Hunting in the snow was ideal, for the dogs' coats blended into the background, making them difficult to spot.

According to the type of terrain on which the dogs lived, there appeared to be a variance of leg lengths. Those living on the grassy Tundra tended to be shorter in the leg than dogs living nearer to the coastal land. The dogs were not always white. There are two groups within the Arctic Spitz family to which the Samoyed belongs. The first group includes the Husky, or Eskimo, dog of Alaska and Canada. The second group includes the true Spitz or Laika group, ranging geographically from Lapland to Kimchatka.

Again this group subdivides, dependent on their tribe, and there are fundamental differences. Some were parti-coloured, black and white, as owned by the Ostiaks, while others were tan, or tan and sable, wolf-grey and red. Some present-day thinking suggests that some of the dogs could even have been Lapphunds. The Samoyeds coming from the Kara and White Sea areas were always white, cream or biscuit-shaded. Basically, therefore, the parti-coloured dogs from southern areas were used mostly as reindeer herders and in the northern parts the white dogs were used as hunting and sledge dogs. A tribe name Bjelkier means white animal that breeds white and this might have made a good alternative name for the breed.

Marion Keyte-Perry believed that Samoyeds developed a breed of dog from the white wolf.

THE EXPLORERS

At the end of the nineteenth century, there were lands still to be fully explored and exciting challenges lay ahead. The major goals at this time were to reach both the north and south poles.

So it was then that the polar explorers set forth armed with sheer zeal and determination to attempt these objectives. Nansen, the Norwegian explorer, in 1893 was probably the first to consider using Samoyeds on a North Pole expedition for pulling heavy loads. He made this decision because it was easier to obtain dogs from North East Russia than it was from Greenland. The Danish Government had put a stop to Eskimo dogs being purchased from the natives, because they were concerned for the well-being of the Eskimo people, who were dependent on having well-trained dogs. The dogs ultimately used by Nansen were a mixed bunch – black and white Ostiak dogs, an odd lop-eared one and others of breed type.

Nansen discovered the Samoyed to be a gentle, loving dog, independently-minded and almost human. Although the Eskimo dogs were stronger and weightier than the smaller Samoyed, and more Samoyeds were necessary for each load, nevertheless the loss of one did not weaken the team to the extent that it would have done with the loss of an Eskimo dog.

Major F. G. Jackson in 1894 was probably the next explorer to use the same breed of dogs on the Jackson-Harmsworth expedition to the North Pole, while C. E. Borchgrevinck was the first to use dog sledges in Antarctica. On his return, some of his dogs were left at Stuart island and these were later used by Shackleton on his Antarctic expedition. Many of the dogs purchased by the explorers were shipped to the central point of Archangel, being temporarily kennelled there with the British Vice-Consul while awaiting collection.

The Duke of Abruzzi, brother to the King of Italy, Captain Scott and the American explorers Fiala and Baldwin, all used Samoyed teams. The hardships endured by these early expedition dogs are just too awful to contemplate. They were mercilessly driven and their feet became torn and bleeding, travelling over hard, encrusted, ridged snow. When they became worn out and exhausted they were killed and fed to the others. On a much more positive note, Etah, who was the explorer Roald Amundsen's lead Samoyed bitch, became the first animal to cross the South Pole on the December 14th 1911.

The dogs were also used by the Russian tax collectors, or Yassak men, who used dog teams in order to collect taxes from people living in snowy wastes. These dogs would travel mile upon mile in the snow maintaining a good steady pace. The dogs would be named for something peculiar about them; for example Laika meant 'barker', Nodka meant 'odd-ball' and Leaneay was 'lazy'.

Although reference is made to explorers identifying two distinct types of Samoyed, it was Mrs Clara Kilburn-Scott who subsequently distinguished and discussed this factor in some detail. Later, other Westerners went on to use Samoyeds commercially and some wonderful stories are told about the dogs in the Arctic.

There is one about a man with a loaded sledge crossing a frozen lake. While running alongside the sledge, he fell through the ice and managed to cling to the ledge. The lead-dog quickly assessed the situation and skewed round suddenly, causing the sledge to overhang the hole. The man was then able to grab the runners and, shouting "mush", was hauled clear of the frozen water.

THE BREED DEVELOPS

Mr Ernest Kilburn-Scott and his wife, Clara, were both members of the Royal Geographical Society. In 1889, Mr Kilburn-Scott was a passenger on a boat which was bound for Archangel on the White Sea. This port became ice-bound during the winter months. On arrival, the boat was loaded with timber and it was during this exercise that Mr Kilburn-Scott noticed some Eskimo-looking men nearby, eating raw fish. He learned that they were of the Samoyed tribe and were from an encampment in the Tundra some miles away.

In order to pass some time, he went with some Russian friends to visit the tribe. There were a lot of dogs running about and he spotted one particular little plump puppy which he bought and eventually brought back to England. This puppy was Sabarka which translates as the 'fat one' in Russian, and was described as being of a dark biscuit colour with white feet.

Sabarka sparked a lot of interest on arrival in England and in 1894 was exhibited in the Foreign dog class in Birmingham. Coincidentally, the Reverend Alex Boddy also bought two Samoyed dogs in Archangel in 1889. Mr Kilburn-Scott then purchased, allegedly from a sailor in London, a Samoyed bitch, Whitey Petchora. Thus in 1896, the Kilburn-Scotts started a breeding programme. They were eventually to use the kennel name of Farningham, but they did also use Polar and Antarctic.

Whitey Petchora was mated to Sabarka but only two puppies were registered at the Kennel Club as Foreign dogs (Samoyeds not being registered as a breed until 1913). The two puppies were named Peter the Great and Neva. Records indicate that Neva, a biscuit-shaded bitch, was bred by Mrs Kilburn-Scott and later owned by Lady Sitwell. Peter the Great, who was black, was sold to the Hon. Mrs McLaren Morrison, who had a great interest in unusual breeds. Early records show that Mrs Morrison actually had four dogs entered in the Foreign class at Crufts in 1903. Since no breed is listed for these dogs and one was called Snow, I can only speculate about whether any of these could have been Samoyeds.

The Dowager Lady Sitwell then purchased Neva from the Kilburn-Scotts and then imported a pure white dog, Musti, from Russia. Neva, bred to Musti, produced the first Champion of the breed, Ch. Olaf Oussa. In 1901, Whitey Petchora was mated to Musti and produced an all-white litter. The famous dog Nansen came out of this litter and another important bitch, Olgalene. On his return from the Jackson-Harmsworth expedition, Major Jackson presented his lead dog, Jacko, to Queen Alexandra and he became a part of the Sandringham Samoyeds, being used as a sire by Mr Kilburn-Scott and other Samoyed breeders.

Flo was Jacko's half-sister. She was mated to Russ, a dog who had been purchased for the Duke of Abruzzi's expedition but for some reason never went. This mating produced a beautiful pure white bitch, Ch. Barena Of Farningham, who was eventually exported to the USA.

Kiev was another bitch who was born on the Jackson-Harmsworth expedition and brought back to England by the ship's doctor. She was mated to Russ. They produced Ch. Pearlene. She was, again, pure white, with rounded ears, and Mr Kilburn-Scott described her as having "a quaint polar-bearish look". Houdin was also an important early dog who was bred to Ch. Pearlene.

ANTARCTIC BUCK
In 1904 Mr Kilburn-Scott took up an appointment at the University of Sydney. He visited the Zoo and there found a young Samoyed, later to be known as Antarctic Buck. It was thought this dog had been born on the ship the *Southern Cross* and had participated in both the Borchgrevinck and Shackleton Expeditions before being eventually left in Australia. Another story suggests he was given away as a puppy to some people in Hobart. Whatever the truth, he ended up at the Zoo.

Later on Mrs Kilburn-Scott visited from England and also promptly visited the Zoo. She offered to buy the dog but the offer was refused. Subsequently, however, it was noticed that the dog was suffering much discomfort from flies and from being chained near two tigers. Again the couple offered to buy him and, this time successful, brought him then to England. Like all imported dogs, he had to go into quarantine but he later joined the Kilburn-Scotts' kennel.

Antarctic Buck was only bred from twice, but his dominance was to prove

Antarctic Nico: This is in display at the Natural History Museum, London, UK.

amazing. Mrs Kilburn-Scott felt it was this factor which improved the Samoyed breed. At ten years of age, after contracting distemper at a show in Redhill, he died. Seven of his puppies survived this epidemic. The two litters he sired were out of Kviklene and out of Ch. Pearlene. His all-male litter from Kviklene produced some of the most influential studs of their day: Southern Cross, Meznit, South Pole, Ch. Fang and Olaf, who was later taken by Captain Scott to the South Pole in 1911.

In 1910, a bitch, Ayesha, was exported from Nova Zembla for Mr Gordon Colman and Mrs Gray Landsberg. There was also the dog Trip from the Borchgrevink expedition, Pelle and Yugor (the lop-eared Sam) from Halfway, Karloff, Sedna from the Scott Antarctic expedition and Rita, another expedition bitch. These dogs carried the most influence in building up the breeding.

It was not until eight strains were produced that the Standard of the breed was drawn up by the Kilburn-Scotts. Antarctic Buck proved an outstanding sire featuring strongly through his two sons, Southern Cross and South Pole, who form the basis of many of today's Samoyeds, having such close noted descendants as Ch. Antarctic Bru Of Farningham, Ch. Kara Sea, Ch. Tiger Boy, Ch. Kosco Of Kobe, Ch. Dimitri Of Kobe, Ch. Silvertips Of Kobe and Ch. Gogolev Corbesky.

BREED RECOGNITION
The Breed was given recognition by The Kennel Club in 1905. At the Ladies

Prince Zoureff.

An early biscuit-shaded dog.

Kennel Association that year the first Challenge Certificate and Best of Breed was awarded by Mr Fred Gresham to Mrs Ringer's Oussa, later to become Ch. Olaf Oussa. In 1909 the original Samoyed Club was founded by all male members. In 1912, the Ladies Samoyed Association was formed. A founder member, Miss M.V. Thompson-Glover obtained her first Samoyed in that year from the Kilburn-Scotts. She became a stalwart of the breed, owning six Champions and one American Champion, including Ch. Eastre and Ch. Eidelweiss. The First World War years followed, when the Kilburn-Scotts moved to Kent. Mrs Kilburn-Scott became the first Secretary of the Samoyed Association.

During the 1920s, when only seven sets of Challenge Certificates were on offer, another outstanding dog was produced, Ch. Kara Sea, bred from Mustan of Farningham and Ch. Zahrina. He won 21 CCs during his

show career, but was also to prove a brilliant stud dog, siring many Champions. Notably, these included Ch. Kara Queen, Am. Ch. Siberian Nansen Of Farningham and Snowland and Eng. & Am. Ch. Tiger Boy Of Norka. The stuffed body of Ch. Siberian Keeno, W.L. Puxley's Samoyed born in 1915, can be seen in the Natural History Museum in London. Keeno won five CCs before being killed in an unfortunate accident.

IMPORTANT EARLY 20TH CENTURY BREEDERS

MARION KEYTE PERRY (ARCTIC)
Marion Keyte Perry's interest in the breed started as a young girl when, in 1924, for a birthday present, she was given a puppy, Fram Of The Arctic. Three years later, she was to acquire a daughter of the famous Ch. Kara Sea. This was Kara Queen, whose 23 Challenge Certificate record was to

Marion Keyte Perry with her Arctic Samoyeds.

stand for some seventy years. In those early days Marion Keyte Perry was instrumental in registering her dogs with her affix Arctic, since Kennel identification names were not extensively used. The only Samoyed she purchased not to bear her affix was Ch. Tchita. In 1929, her first home-bred Champion was Ch. White Rover Of The Arctic (Ch. Loga Of The Arctic ex Ch. Winter). A painting of Ch. Loga Of The Arctic hangs in the Kennel Club today. She was to export stock to many parts of the world. Her second English Champion was exported to New Zealand and became Eng. NZ Ch. Rex of the Arctic.

Marion Keyte Perry, who was Principal of a girls' school, employed a kennel manager, Mrs Smith, who looked after the forty dogs and bitches in the kennel at its peak. The last litter was bred in 1959. Marion Keyte Perry was President of the British Samoyed Club for 21 years and was a Chairperson of the Ladies Kennel Club. She was to own, in all, seventeen Champions and was very concerned about having pure white coats. She died in 1967.

MRS D. L. PERRY (KOBE)
It was 1926 that Mrs Perry obtained two Samoyeds from Mrs Kilburn-Scott – a bitch, Chia, and a dog Polki who unfortunately died of distemper. Mr and Mrs Perry already held the affix Kobe since they previously owned Pekingese. Their first litter was born in 1928, sired by Nadir, and produced ten puppies. Their first Champion was to be Ch. Kosca Of Kobe.

Many, many illustrious Champions were to follow on over the ensuing years, Ch. Peter, Ch. Dimitri, Ch. Prince Bado, Ch. White Fang, Ch. Zeeta, Ch. Karabelle, Ch. Sleigh King, Ch. Sleigh Monarch, Ch. Sleigh Leader, all of Kobe – to name but a few! The name became associated with quality, and particularly famous dogs exported world-wide were Am. Ch. Americ Of Kobe, Aust. Ch. Starya Of Kobe, Aust. Ch. Icemist Beauty Of Kobe and Aust. NZ Ch. Tatina Of Kobe.

The most successful of Mrs Perry's dogs in the UK was Eng. Irish Ch. Gogolev Corbesky (see Chapter Eight 'Record breakers'). Although this dog did not bear the Kobe affix, his father was Ch. Whitestar Of Kobe. Today, Kobe dogs are still talked about and revered. Their heads especially were known to be good. Mrs Perry herself was always immaculate whenever she showed or judged, perfectly complementing her dogs, especially with her white hair. She would arrive at a show with her chauffeur who was also smartly dressed in a green livery. The kennel was active for 47 years, with Irene Ashfield, her daughter, taking over the reins during the 1950s. In all, 44 Champions emerged. Mrs Perry became President of the Samoyed Association in 1949, remaining in office for 14 years, when she was succeeded by her daughter. She died in 1970.

ADA L. WESTCOTT (SNOWLAND)
Ada Westcott first acquired a Samoyed she named Joan as a pet for her invalid son. This Samoyed died of distemper. Following the later tragic death of her son, Ada was given Christina Marie, a bitch of Kobe breeding, who was born in 1933. This bitch was very thin but was mated to a local Samoyed, Taz. This litter was to include two future Champions in Ch. Bettina Marie, who

was retained, and French Ch. Julian Jim, who was owned by the Count de Savignac and became a World Champion in 1936. Christina Marie went on to become a CC winner.

Mrs Westcott was born in Devon of farming stock and had a good knowledge of pedigrees and breeding. She owned one of the great kennels and was active in the breed for over thirty years, registering her kennel name in 1937. Her main breeding lines were from the Kilburn-Scotts' Farningham lines. While the Kobe kennel specialised in head and expression, the Snowland dogs were known for their dense and harsh coats. Ch. Snowland Marda was a biscuit-coloured bitch and won nine CCs. A later kennel based most closely to Snowland was Rose Lewis's Snowcryst kennel.

Mrs Westcott exported stock mainly to the USA, but also to Canada, Holland, France, Norway, South Africa and Australia. Many Champions in those countries came from her stock. She was not able to show extensively, due to the remoteness of her home.

As there was already a Snowland affix in the USA, Martingate was added to distinguish between the two kennels – Martingate being the name of her house. One of the main sires exported to the USA was Martingate Snowland Taz, later to become an American Champion.

Mrs Westcott usually kept eight to ten Samoyeds at a time, mainly bitches. Only one dog was kept at a time because of fights. She was able to continue her breeding programme during the war years since she lived near a slaughterhouse, from where she was able to obtain a good supply of food for the dogs. It was in 1955 that Mrs Wescott judged the breed at Crufts. The last

Snowland litter was born in 1963. Mrs Wescott died in 1980 at the wonderful age of ninety-one years.

SAMOYEDS USA

Princess de Montyglyon exhibited dogs at shows in Europe. She was born a Belgian Countess and married a lion-tamer. In 1902, she was given a Samoyed, the Russian Ch. Moustan Of Argenteau, by Grand Duke Nicholas. When she came to live in America in 1904, she brought all her dogs with her, including four Samoyeds. Ch. Moustan Of Argenteau thus became the first Samoyed to be registered in America. That was in 1906. The other three Samoyeds were Martyska, Sora and Siberia Of Argenteau. In 1907, Moustan's son, Ch. Witte Of Argenteau, was to become the first American Champion. Siberia became a Champion in 1908.

Around this time Mrs Ada van Hensen also became interested in the breed and imported two bitches. One of them, Tamara, became the first American Samoyed bitch Champion. She was mated to a son of Moustan, called Czarevitch, and produced Ch. Zuroff. Moustan was also the sire of Ch. Greenacre Kieff and Evalo. In turn, Kieff was the grandson of Ch. Fang Of Yurok, Ch. Kazon Of Yurok and Ch. Zanoza.

Many people then began to obtain Samoyeds. Mrs Elizabeth Hudson joined the ranks. Some years later, one of the dogs she imported from the UK was Ch. Stormcloud. In 1914, a young schoolgirl, Ruth Nicholls, was given a Samoyed as a birthday present. This bitch, Wiemur, was to make a real impact on the breed. However, she was not registered until 1918. Bred to Czarevitch, she produced

Ch. Malshick and Ch. Shut Balackeror. This second dog was used as a foundation stud for Mrs Frank Romer's Yukak Kennels. Czarevitch had proved to be an influential sire during this early period.

Mrs Romer then imported Tobalsk to her kennels, later to become Ch. Tobalsk. He proved to be a marvellous sire and was to become one of the greatest Samoyeds of all time in America. Undoubtedly he improved the type.

A mating to a bitch, Otiska, produced some good show winners, including Ch. Toby Of Yurak II who won BOB at the Westminster Dog Show. Tobalsk's sister, Ch. Draga, was imported at the same time. Mated to Ch. Shut Balackeror and Zev Of Yurak, she produced Champions. In 1937, the Yurak Kennels were transferred to Eddie Barbean.

In 1920, Miss Mildred Trevor Sheridan started her Park-Cliffe Kennels with a Russian import, Hasova. In 1921 the OBI Kennels of F. L. Vinton and the Norka Kennels of Mr and Mrs Reid were founded.

In 1929 the Reids imported the famous Ch. Tiger Boy, son of the equally famous Eng. Ch. Kara Sea.

Other famous names of this era included Mr and Mrs Seeley of the Donerna Kennels. They imported, from England, a dog who was to become Ch. Donerna's Barin.

This dog was a descendant of Antarctic Buck. He had an amazing influence on the breed, producing well over a hundred progeny. Two other famous kennels were Wingbrook and Top o' the World.

THE SAMOYED CLUB OF AMERICA
On February 14th 1923, following the Westminster Show, a meeting was held and the proposed Samoyed Club of America adopted the English standard. The Club was approved by the American Kennel Club that May. At this time there were around three hundred Samoyeds in America. The Club President was Mrs A.E. Mason and the Secretary Mrs Dolly Ward.

THE FAMOUS 'N' LITTER
The very first Specialty Show was held at Tuxedo in 1929. BOB was Tiger Boy Of Norka under the then Club President, Mr Louis Smirnow. Tiger Boy had just been imported from England. In 1929, Elizabeth Hudson's imported Ch. Snowcloud sired Vida Of Snowland, who was to become a foundation bitch for Helen Harris of Pennsylvania. The Snowland Kennel became widely respected and Helen Harris visited England and imported quality stock from the Arctic and Farningham Kennels. From the latter she obtained Sabarka Of Farningham, and two puppies by Ch. Kara Sea ex Pinky Of Farningham. One of the puppies was named Siberian Nansen Of Farningham And Snowland. Unfortunately, his sister, Martyska Of Farningham, died at a very early age.

Nansen, however, proved to be a remarkable stud dog. Out of Vida Of Snowland was produced a very famous litter, to become known as the 'N' litter. Nadya, Nianya, Nikita, Nim and Norna all became Champions. This was an incredible litter – and Mrs Harris became admired for parting with outstanding bitches to other parts of the USA. Later, she imported Ice Crystal Of The Arctic. Among Nansen's progeny was a dog, Ch. Starvyna Of Snowland, who was to be owned by Bob and Dolly Ward of California, co-authors of *The New Samoyed*.

US BREED EXPANSION

From the late 1930s, Mrs Agnes Mason and her White Way Kennels were to make an enormous contribution to the breed in the USA. Mrs Mason was brought up in Alaska where her father worked sled dogs. She bought in stock from both England and the USA. She imported Silver Spark Of The Arctic and Eng. Ch. Whiteway Of Kobe. Together with her daughter, she was to own 14 Champions and to breed 22. Her sled dog team gained much publicity and one of her most famous dogs was Ch. Rex Of Whiteway.

During the 1930s Juliet Goodrich founded the Snowshoe Hill Kennels. She worked to help eradicate hip dysplasia and did much to research and record the breed in the USA. Around 1937, Samoyeds started to take part in Obedience at shows, the first Samoyed

winner being Ch. Alstasia's Rukavitza CD owned by Mrs Anastasia MacBain.

During the war years, all activities were severely limited. There was a Breed Specialty in 1941 but with only a small entry, and not another one until 1946. However, in 1943, another outstanding dog started to emerge. He was Ch. Starchak CD, bred by the Masons. He was to be owned by Bob and Dolly Ward. He was to sire 16 Champions and become grandfather to numerous Champions. He won 32 BOBs and was the Wimunstrev Top Stud Dog Winner in 1956. He died in 1957. Bob and Dolly Ward were to become legends in their own lifetime. As well as breeding and exhibiting, they became trainers and took part in Obedience and sled dog racing. They supported local clubs, and both held the office of President of the Samoyed Club of America during the 1960s. Bob was also a member of the Breed Standards Committee in 1956. Both became highly respected and they judged all over the world.

3 THE SAMOYED PUPPY

First ask yourself if this is the right breed for you, your family and your lifestyle. Read up as much as you can on the breed. Samoyeds do make excellent pets, adore young children and possess a loving and mischievous nature. However, you do need to devote time and energy to a growing Samoyed. It is a commitment not to be lightly undertaken since it must be for the whole lifetime of the dog. If you are now finally convinced that this is the breed for you, the next logical step would be to find out where to purchase a puppy.

FINDING A BREEDER

My advice would be to resist the lure of pet shops or any commercial kennels and try to find a small private breeder. Try and imagine where stock for some commercial establishments might originate from. Any breeder worth their salt would strive to produce quality stock and would certainly not pass on any puppies without personally securing happy and loving homes for them. Such a breeder would offer sound and sensible advice and would be willing to be at the end of a phone-line day or night if you should require further help and support. There is no doubt you

would be put through a strict vetting procedure – but that it is to be welcomed.

So where should you now look? There are various avenues you can pursue. A list of people who have currently registered a litter can be supplied by the Kennel Club. Breeders registering puppies can pay a small additional sum to have their names included on such a list. The only problem with this is that 'puppy farmers' do creep in. You need to run these names by someone in the know. You can also obtain from your national Kennel Club the names of Breed Club Secretaries or you could contact the Breed Clubs direct. From that source, additional information can be obtained. Another alternative is to purchase the dog newspapers and magazines. Finally, of course, you could always visit a dog show and speak with any exhibitors you would find there.

VISITING A BREEDER

When you have obtained the names and details of a few breeders, telephone them and introduce yourself. Inform the breeder that you are considering buying a Samoyed and ask if you could come along for a chat. I never consider myself to be wasting time on visitors who are anxious

The appeal of a Samoyed puppy is hard to resist, but think carefully before taking on the commitment of owning a dog.

to have a puppy but might be deliberating between two or three breeds. To my mind this is a sensible course of action to take, to gather all possible information before making a choice. It matters not if eventually that choice is for another breed of dog.

DOG OR BITCH?

This is a question most frequently put to me. Should I choose a dog or a bitch? My answer is to simply point out the implications of the difference between the two sexes and stress to the purchasers that the decision is ultimately theirs to make.

The dog is larger, stronger and, like most male species, more strikingly attractive than the female. Because of

'pulling' tendencies on the lead, the strength of the male should be taken into account.

The bitch, on the other hand, is normally easier to handle, given the fact that she is smaller and less strong. There is the problem of a bitch coming into heat or season every six months, which can be off-putting to some. One solution would be to have the bitch spayed, unless you are planning to show her.

There is simply no truth in the old saying that a bitch is more faithful than a dog. In the Samoyed breed, the males are equally loving and affectionate. It may be worth considering Breed Rescue and giving thought to offering a Samoyed in need a good home. Many are referred, through no fault of their own, and are still young and healthy. Examples of these circumstances include a divorcing couple or a mum expecting a baby who can no longer cope with a dog as well.

CHOOSING A PUPPY

Inevitably Samoyed puppies sell themselves, so to a certain extent they are their own worst enemy. For visitors to big multi-breed commercial kennels, the sight of a little white bundle of fluff with eyes like two blackcurrants peeping through kennel bars is irresistible. Enough for an instant purchase to be made without having full information on the breed and making a considered judgement. Nevertheless, let us hope that all aspects have been fully taken into account and that you are now going to choose a puppy from a well-bred litter.

For a start, there is no point at all in going to see the puppies before four weeks of age. Only then do they start to develop fully with individual characteristics. On viewing the puppies at this age, you may well favour one which appeals to you as against the others. Returning the next day, it would be a fair assumption that you would not be able to identify the same puppy again unless a little identifying mark was made on the tummy.

No doubt a decision will have been taken on your part as to whether the puppy was to be shown or required simply as a pet. Indeed you could be persuaded to show. In any event it is all down to finer points and it could be that a puppy sold as a pet, or the last of a litter, turns out to be the best of the lot on reaching maturity. This is the reason breeders will 'run puppies on' to see how they develop at a later age. Do also be guided by advice from the breeder. If you are offered just one particular puppy, ensure that you see the whole litter just to compare. Also if you are wanting a 'show off' for the show ring do not consider choosing a shy puppy sitting in a corner.

ASSESSING A PUPPY

The puppy will normally be allowed to leave the breeder at seven or eight weeks of age. By this time, a good wedge-shaped head should have developed. Do not consider anything looking too snipy (narrow and pointed). Look for a 'Mongolian slant' to the eyes. Any discharge coming from the corner may indicate a blocked tear duct. The ears could still be folded at this age, but check the thickness. Assess that the puppy seems to have plenty of good bone. Look for a firm, well-curled tail.

Watch the puppies playing together so you can get an indication of their individual personalities.

The breeder will help you to assess show potential.

You will be able to see what type of coat the growing puppy will possess by looking at the parents. Check the movement by watching the puppy moving across the floor with the littermates or, if you are deliberating between two, have them move singly. Look at pigmentation on the rims of eyes and mouth. Some people might require a puppy to be fully 'blacked up' before purchasing, i.e. ensuring that pigmentation is totally black. If some pink is showing, experience shows, more often than not, that in time this will fill in. I once acquired a puppy, whose pigmentation on half of one side of her mouth was totally pink. I gambled that this gap would fill in and it did. As far as colour is concerned, you may have an individual preference for white, but remember cream and biscuit are equally acceptable. I once received a panic-stricken telephone call from a lady who said she had purchased a puppy, but that when she bathed it she found that it had brown ears. She thought she had been sold a crossbreed. I assured the lady all was normal: many Samoyeds have biscuit-coloured ears, seen especially when wet.

PRICE AND TERMS

When you have made your ultimate choice, you need to pay the breeder for the puppy. Most breeders will charge the same for a 'pet' and for a show puppy because what you are actually buying is a correctly bred, healthy puppy of quality. If the puppy does make it in the show ring, this is an added extra. You are now free to take your puppy home – and your life will never be the same again.

GOING HOME

After you have purchased your Samoyed puppy, you may well have to undertake a long car ride before reaching home. Take a towel or small cardboard box to place in your lap and get someone else to do the driving. In most instances, the puppy will take the car ride in its stride, since rarely are Samoyeds car-sick.

THE FIRST NIGHT

Arriving at his new home, the puppy will wish to explore and investigate a whole new world. The first night, prepare yourself for the fact that the puppy may cry in these strange surroundings without his littermates. Decide beforehand where he is going to sleep and stick to your decision. If you take the puppy into the bedroom you are making a rod for your own back since he will always want to sleep there. Take him to where you wish him to sleep and leave him. A cursory check of his well-being can be made during the night.

Do not bother buying a fancy basket, he will probably chew that to bits. A piece of fleecy-type bedding in a puppy pen is probably ideal, but invariably the puppy will ignore this and push it to one side. Of course, if you do have another dog, this

Most pups feel a little lost when they first arrive in their new home.

is a great help because the puppy will cuddle alongside.

HEALTH CHECK

Make arrangements for your vet to give the puppy a health check the day after arriving home and arrange for vaccinations. The puppy will be covered by immunity through mum's milk for up to twelve weeks, but will eventually need to be inoculated against hardpad, distemper, parvovirus etc. For more details on vaccinations and worming refer to Chapter Ten on Health.

BEING CONSISTENT

From day one be consistent with the puppy. If he is to respect you he needs firmness and discipline blended with kindness. His daily care should involve looking after his mental as well as his physical needs, and it is not reasonable to leave a young puppy, or even an older dog, caged up for hours on end in a kitchen while you are out working. A crate can be useful, but only for containing a puppy for short periods of time. If you leave the door open, he will accept it as his secure place. You will also find crates useful for the back of a car so that a puppy, or any dog, is not thrown around.

It is important to decide where in your home the puppy will be allowed to wander so that he becomes aware of his limits and does not cause damage. Consider using a puppy pen or even a gate across the kitchen door. Try not to fall into the temptation of giving in to the puppy, making him spoilt. One of the big advantages of the Samoyed breed is that there is no 'doggy odour', so this is a real bonus if the puppy or dogs are kept in the house.

Puppyhood is a time to enjoy, but it is important to be consistent in your training so that your Samoyed understands what is acceptable behaviour.

CORRECTING BAD BEHAVIOUR

Should you own a number of dogs who might sleep out in a kennel, only allow the puppy to go with them at three to four months. The puppy will probably want to follow them anyway. Teach the puppy to respond to the word "No" if caught doing something he should not be doing, such as chewing cupboard doors. You might even wish to shake the ruff with both hands while saying this. This would happen naturally in the wild, with older Samoyed dogs correcting a young one. A rolled-up newspaper can be used as another method of correction. Do not hit out with your hand because this will upset the puppy and he will fail to understand. Just a gentle tap on the nose or the sound of newspaper on the nearest wall surface will make him take notice. Should a puppy try to gnaw your hand, just return the pressure and he will soon stop. If you adhere to these instructions, you will have commenced your own training programme and should be on the right track.

HOUSE TRAINING

Individual puppies do vary in adaptability. There is no specific length of time involved. Get into the habit of letting the puppy out into the garden at regular intervals, and especially after a sleep or a meal, to empty out. A young puppy cannot control his bladder and food places extra pressure on this. Encourage the puppy, by use of a word he will come to understand, for example 'wee' or 'go'. If a puppy has to relieve himself in the house, put down plenty of newspaper. When cleaning up, retain the bottom sheet and place it on top of some new sheets, so that the paper will retain the scent and the puppy will know where to go. Place by the door.

SAFETY PRECAUTIONS

I have found that there is one golden rule with Samoyed puppies – never underestimate them and always try to be one jump ahead of them all the time. I refer, of course, to destructive chewing. If you have to leave the puppy for any length of time, check to see that everything is secure, especially that no doors can be opened to other parts of the house. Look to see what he could possibly find to chew and remove it if at all feasible. I am referring to such items as loose mats, rubbish bins and items within reach of the table and work surfaces. Believe me, a puppy will manage to find something you have overlooked. Our first Samoyed managed to retrieve my handbag off the kitchen table overnight. I came down in the morning to find the contents in shreds, including a wallet and four £5 notes. Luckily the bank replaced them! In any room of the house, do be careful with electric cord. One evening a venturesome young puppy managed to find a two-inch flex between the rear of the freezer and the plug, and proceeded to chew. Luckily he was caught in time and another important lesson was learned.

FEEDING
The breeder of your puppy will no doubt have provided you with a diet sheet which should prove invaluable. You will probably also have received a small amount of the food. In order to avoid any stomach upsets, you should continue with this diet, making any changes you might require gradually. Do be very careful in the administering of food to a young puppy.

Overfeeding can cause diarrhoea, while also putting excess strain on a young and growing frame. It is all too easy to ruin the front of a young puppy by excess weight. It is always best therefore to slightly underfeed. Also do not leave uneaten food down, because it becomes unpalatable. Fresh drinking water should continually be supplied. Your puppy may well turn out to be one of the mischievous ones who delight in overturning water bowls, even walking off with them, leaving the kitchen floor awash. It might be useful to know that you can purchase a specially designed dish which will not up-end.

When the puppy reaches six months of age he will require only two meals per day until he reaches the age of twelve months.

You must then decide whether you wish to continue feeding two smaller meals or just feed one large meal daily. If you do just feed one large meal daily, a few bedtime treats, such as a few biscuits, will not come amiss. The teeth of your puppy will change between four and six months. Sometimes teeth can be seen to drop out onto the carpet, but again this is quite normal. During this time you may notice the puppy going through what is known as 'the monkey stage'. The face will very much resemble the face of a monkey. Usually by six months, this has disappeared and the puppy will once more be back in proportion.

By nine months, the puppy will appear to be getting thinner. This is due to loss of puppy fat and rapid growth. A puppy bitch will usually start to lose her coat at this stage.

Teething can be a difficult time, and it is helpful if you provide chews and safe toys for your puppy.

LEASH TRAINING

Introduce the puppy to a collar and leash as soon as possible. I usually start by putting a collar on the puppy for short periods of time, then introducing the leash a couple of days later. Use a leather roll collar for a Samoyed puppy. This will not damage the ruff. Limit sessions up and down the garden to just a few minutes each day, initially. After much scratching, leaping and general merriment, it will gradually dawn on the puppy what is expected of him.

Sometimes a puppy will just sit down and refuse to budge. Exercise patience so that when he eventually does start to move again you can talk to him and praise him. In order to teach the puppy to come to you, just gently pull the leash towards yourself saying "Come" or "Here". Samoyeds do have a natural tendency to pull while on a leash. This can be corrected by use of a 'halti' which fits around the muzzle of a dog, rather than being attached to the collar. The 'halti' comes in various sizes and can be purchased from a vet or pet shop. It is very useful and is often used by owners of strong adult Samoyed dogs when going to shows.

EXERCISE

Samoyed puppies need little exercise until six months. Although it is important that your puppy is socialised with the outside world as soon as possible, do try to refrain from taking the puppy on long walks. Be sensible and just gradually increase the walking distance. To muscle up a Samoyed puppy too young will do his movement no good. Allow your puppy daily free romps in your garden, which he will physically enjoy and which will add to his mental well-being.

TRAINING FOR GROOMING

From the moment you acquire your puppy, learn to place him on a grooming table with a non-slip surface, just for a few minutes each day. Your breeder will no doubt have already carried out this exercise with the puppy. Hold him very carefully or get a second person to hold him, while you gently brush him. If the puppy seems to wriggle and object, just be firm and calm. Talk to him reassuringly and praise him for standing still. Build up the grooming time slowly as the puppy gets used to the routine. Daily grooming is essential to keep the coat clean and free from knots and tangles and it also stimulates new growth.

You will need to purchase a bristle, nylon or wire brush and a rounded-tooth comb, one half being finer than the other. Choice of brush should be made wisely, since some wire brushes have a tendency

Start grooming at an early stage, and your Samoyed will soon learn to accept the routine.

to pull out undercoat. Obviously, at a tender age, you will need a small brush for a baby puppy. As the puppy gets a few weeks older and the coat grows profusely, train him to stand on the table four-square. Place your arms completely round his legs and pull towards you so that the youngster is now lying in the resting position. Stroke the puppy's tummy gently, it will help him to relax.

Starting at the head, part the coat with the back of the left hand in small sections and brush and comb towards you, gradually moving down the length of the body from the roots. Take particular care round the sensitive parts. On completing one side, stand the puppy and turn him round to enable you to do the other side. He will eventually learn to turn himself around for you. Brush the tail well before attempting to comb out. Many dogs, in particular, are touchy about their back ends. When you have thoroughly combed both sides, stand the puppy, giving the same close attention to the ruff area under the chin downwards. If a dog continually wears a collar this is an area that tends to mat very easily.

Comb the skirts (bitches) or trousers (dogs) again, parting the sections away as before with the left hand. Allow the tail to naturally fall over the back and brush and comb from the tip to the base. Brush the tail at the base into the trousers/skirts. With the fine part of the comb pay attention to the ears, especially the base, which very easily can get lumpy, also the elbows, hocks and featherings. Finally, give the puppy a good all-over brushing.

BATHING
Do not bother to bath your puppy until absolutely necessary, unless you are showing. If you have a muddy, smelly puppy, bathing will be necessary. Dry the puppy very carefully with a towel, because young puppies cannot cope with being wet, and then blow-dry with a hair dryer. The puppy will not like this at first but will gradually get used to it. Some breeders still use a block of soap for bathing, which cleanses and enhances whiteness, but these days there are endless choices of dog shampoo. Always check teeth and brush them with dog toothpaste on a weekly basis.

THE COAT
Generally speaking, a Samoyed puppy will hold coat until ten months of age, when it will start to 'blow' and will need to be combed out completely. As a rough guide, a Samoyed dog will cast his coat once a year and a bitch possibly twice. It is essential that the coat is removed as quickly as possible, because if this is not done it will tangle and become lumpy. It is not unusual for the coat to start to go in patches, for example on the legs or neck, and there can be a partial or complete moult. The dog will look thin but there is nothing wrong.

Groom the dog, removing loose hair. Bath and groom again. Bathing will loosen the coat which will now come away quite easily. After a bitch has had a litter of puppies, she will frequently drop her coat to the extent that all her black and pink pigmentation can be clearly seen. This is all perfectly normal. The sooner a 'blowing coat' is combed out, the sooner it will grow back in, with new clean white growth pushing through thicker each day. Many Samoyed owners collect the hair from their dog, so that it can be spun when a large amount is obtained.

4 THE ADULT SAMOYED

After twelve months, the chubby puppy will grow into a leggier, sleeker adult. This is another stage of growth; the youngster is no longer a puppy and yet not quite an adult. At this stage an adolescent sometimes becomes a little finicky about food. Bitches, even more so than dogs, tend to drop coat, making them less attractive. Personally, I am always glad when the two-year marker has been reached, because then you can see the completed Samoyed. Do remember to worm adolescents regularly (see Chapter 10: Health Care). But now we can move on to the adult Samoyed.

FEEDING
I would recommend that the adult Samoyed be fed on two smaller meals, given morning and evening, rather than

Actress Beverley Callard with her Samoyeds. The adult dog needs a planned regime of feeding, exercise and grooming to maintain top condition. Photo: Holborn Picture Agency.

GROOMING YOUR SAMOYED
Groomer Lyn Dutton.

1. A Samoyed that has been trained to go on a grooming table from puppyhood will be happy and relaxed.

2. Start working through the coat with a brush.

3. As you work through the coat, lift it layer by layer, so you get right down to the skin.

4. The tail needs special attention to ensure a lovely plume.

5. When you are working on the undercarriage, it is easier if your Samoyed lies down.

6. A comb is used on the hair behind the ears, which mats and tangles very easily.

7. Comb through the feathering on the forelegs.

8. The hair on the back legs needs attention as does the rear feathering.

9. A pin brush is used to fluff up the coat. This is often used as a last-minute preparation before going in the show ring.

having one large meal. This aids digestion. Avoid giving treats, but give a couple of biscuits at bedtime. The choice of food is now down to your own preference.

Nowadays, as well as raw meat, there is really so much choice of prepared foods – complete diets, biscuits, canned meat, moist simulated ground-meat food, etc. Most foods are divided into categories, for example, Puppy, Junior, Maintenance, Active. An adult dog should fall into the Maintenance category, or Active if it is a working or racing dog. Remember to add some chopped green vegetables and some fish oil to the diet. Whatever you do, never overfeed. Your Samoyed will decide for himself how much food he wishes to eat. Pick up the dish when he has finished feeding. If it is left down, he may return for a few more bites, but snacking during the day will just spoil his appetite for the next meal. Feed a marrow bone occasionally, but certainly not chicken or chop bones, which will splinter. Bones aid digestion, dogs enjoy them and they also help keep teeth and gums in good condition. It is better for the dog to gnaw the bone rather than to eat it because, if this happens, constipation can occur. Always leave fresh water down.

GROOMING
An adult dog will grow a more dense and profuse coat. It is essential that your Samoyed be kept clean. A five-minute brush each day will rid the coat of any mud or dust and stimulate coat growth. It will also provide you with the opportunity to check for any external parasites (see Chapter Ten on Health).

Allow more time for a weekly groom. Use a grooming table rather than sitting on the floor and getting backache. Lie the dog on his side and comb him from head to tail, ensuring that the comb reaches right down to the skin, as the coat is parted layer by layer.

Remember to pay regular attention to teeth and nails. Ensure that the teeth are kept free from the build-up of tartar by regular brushing. If this is not done, this brown and hard composition will form close to the gums. Scaling is then necessary to remove it, which usually requires a visit to the vet and, probably, an anaesthetic.

If the dog is kept exercised on hard ground this will cause the nails to wear so trimming will not be necessary. However, if trimming is required, this should be done with nail clippers and not scissors.

EXERCISE
All dogs look forward to their daily walks, and exercise is essential. They also like routine. An adult Samoyed should be given a minimum of two half-hour walks per day. The Samoyed will pull very strongly on the lead when out walking unless he is well controlled. This is where a 'halti', which is a head collar, can come in useful. It is specially designed, in strong nylon, to prevent pulling. Any pet shop should be able to help with size and fitting.

A free run over fields plus some roadwork is ideal for enjoyment and maintenance of muscle. An extended lead is a useful item for exercising dogs these days. If more than one Samoyed is owned and the dogs are exercised together, there is occasionally a tendency for one to lead another astray when allowed to run free. Believe me, they all have different traits which you need to

THE FAMILY DOG

Try to include your Samoyeds in as many outings as possible.

A day out at the beach is a source of great enjoyment.

A big family expedition – but these Australian Samoyeds are perfectly behaved.

It's all part of the fun of owning a long-coated white dog!

gauge. Many are just plain biddable and will stay with you. If not, with two, it is a good idea to let one run free, keeping the other on the extended lead, changing them round halfway through the exercise. We had one Samoyed bitch who was as good as gold free-running for most of the time, then just 'bolted' if something took her attention. Calling her back just fell on deaf ears.

Do not confine your Samoyed for long periods without providing compensating exercise and play. Do remember to clean up after your dog when walking in the street or park.

IDENTIFICATION

Do provide identification for your Samoyed at all times. This is usually done by means of a name tag attached to a collar, or you might wish to consider microchipping. This is achieved by injecting an implant under the skin between the dog's shoulder blades. Registration is made with a relevant organisation. When the dog has been found, having strayed, been lost or been stolen, he can then be scanned and identified.

ADULT BEHAVIOUR

As the Samoyed matures he should become even more manageable. Puppy chewing activities should have ceased. Now is the time for a reappraisal of the situation, to ensure that you have instilled a firm routine and the necessary discipline. Do not let your dog dictate to you; you must act as pack leader and set boundaries, as you would do with a child. Do not allow your dog to jump on your furniture or all over people as they enter your home. Just the tone of your voice and a firm "No" or "Down" should be all that is required to correct him. Your Samoyed should, by this stage, know what is acceptable and what is not.

Sometimes, often through boredom, a Samoyed might chew his front paws or tail. A preparation such as 'Bitter Apple'

A well-trained, well-socialised adult will be a pleasure to own.
Photo: Paulo Defelippi.

applied to the spot will prevent this – but you must also ask yourself "Why is my dog bored?"

If something does occur that you really do not know how to cope with, seek advice either from your breeder, any Samoyed Breed Club Secretary or committee member, or your vet. Consider neutering for any aggressive behaviour in males.

Many breed clubs and National Kennel Clubs have introduced a form of Good Citizen Scheme in order to encourage responsible ownership and, ultimately, a well-controlled dog.

All Samoyeds, whether they are to be kept as pets, as show dogs, as working dogs or as dogs to have fun with, must be properly trained. Do go to training and socialisation classes – and then you will have been true to your Samoyed.

NEUTERING

The best time for a bitch to be neutered (spayed) is two or three months after her first heat period. By then she should be mentally and physically mature. This can be undertaken to prevent her coming into season, to prevent unwanted puppies or for certain medical conditions. It is achieved by surgical removal of the ovaries. Recovery is usually quite speedy.

Although it is thought that spayed bitches put on weight, these bitches actually require less food, so it is overfeeding which causes the weight gain. The bitch's coat will become quite dense and profuse. Spayed bitches can be shown but require Kennel Club permission.

A male can be neutered at any age. The usual reason is to prevent the siring of pups, or if a male becomes aggressive.

The aggression is due to the hormone testosterone, which is responsible for male characteristics and which is found in the testes. The operation involves the removal of the testicles. After the operation the male usually becomes more docile and loses his sexual drive. Again there is a tendency for obesity, so restrict food input. Following the operation the dog will develop a heavy, profuse coat, making grooming difficult.

THE VETERAN SAMOYED
Your Samoyed will age in much the same way as you do. There may be deafness, or weakness of eyes, cataracts may

Ch. Ostyak Snow Princess: An eleven-year old Samoyed, still looking at the peak of health and fitness.

develop and there can be wastage of muscles, or even incontinence. There is a tendency for the dog to become less active and it is essential to prevent obesity through appropriate exercise and a low-calorie diet. Feed a little wheatgerm to avoid constipation. Supplement food with vitamins. The Vitamin B complex is known as the age-fighter. On average, a Samoyed can live up to twelve or thirteen years – sixteen years old has been known.

The older dog will feel the cold, so ensure that a blanket or Vetbed is provided on which to sleep. Let your dog out into the garden more frequently. Offer extra love and affection. I am convinced that many older dogs survive on tender loving care. One of my oldies did. Refusing to eat on her own, she was spoon-fed B. Sorb and Complan daily and given plenty of love and attention. She survived for five months like this before departing from us.

It is sometimes kinder to have a beloved companion put to sleep rather than to let them suffer with no quality of life. A vet might even agree to visit your home to administer a final injection. It is the last service, which only you can decide on, for your faithful Samoyed. Eventually the passage of time will enable you to cope with your grief by remembering the wonderful times your shared together. No-one can take these from you.

5 THE VERSATILE SAMOYED

Not all owners of Samoyeds are merely obsessed by their beauty. There are many people who love their working ability and wish to preserve this aspect of the breed, which they regard as being fundamental to the Samoyed's character. Many Samoyeds are now living in countries, and in environments, where there are no reindeer to herd, but that is no reason why they should be bred just to become wonderful show pieces. In this chapter four experts describe their experiences and opinions about promoting the working instincts of the Samoyed.

THE SAMOYED IN NORTH AMERICA

Pam Landers is the Chair of the Samoyed Club of American Working Committee and gives advice not only about the work that Samoyeds are doing but also about the interest their owners derive from watching them doing it.

THE WORKING SAMOYED IN AMERICA

By Pam Landers
The historians of our breed tell us that Samoyeds served their nomadic human companions in a variety of ways. Their versatility as herders, draft animals, pack animals, hunters, and friends is rare in the canine world of selective breeding. Because of the many talents and skills this versatility requires, the original Samoyed was intelligent, strong, and agile. Though many people are drawn to Samoyeds because of their breathtaking beauty, a few have been strongly attracted by their working abilities as well; indeed, the dogs came to western Europe because of their hardiness and talents as sled pullers.

The breeders of Samoyeds who have attempted to maintain these working abilities recognise that, without the ability to do their jobs, Samoyeds are only the outer shell of their former selves. In the United States a few people have worked with their Samoyeds for as long as the breed has been here. For the most part, these working Sams have been sled dogs.

In the early 1980s a number of these people coalesced into an informal group called the Organisation for Working Samoyeds in order to learn from each

47

other and to honour good working dogs. In the beginning they provided certificates of achievement in two areas, sled racing and weight pull. This group persuaded the breed parent club, the Samoyed Club of America (SCA), to include sled dog and sled bitch classes in the National Samoyed Specialty to showcase those dogs.

In the early 1990s, SCA members began to express concern for the future of the breed's working abilities, fearing the split into "show" and "working" dogs that has plagued many another breed. In addition, Robert Ward, patriarch of the breed in America, made clear that, although the Samoyed Club of America had about 1000 members at the time, his most recent book had sold many, many more copies, indicating that far more Sammy owners were not members of the club than were. These were people who were not caught up in the conformation showing world, but who were captivated by the breed enough to want to share their lives with these dogs.

In order to highlight and support the Sammy working abilities, while providing Sammy owners not involved in conformation a reason to become part of the Samoyed Club of America community, the parent club formed a committee to create a Working Certification programme. The committee wanted to create a programme that gave credit for any work a Samoyed could do that was not already recognised by the American Kennel Club; and to provide incentives for people living almost anywhere to work with their dogs.

The committee devised a programme that would give working degrees to dogs that earned points by means of race

sledding, excursion sledding, weight pull, pack hiking, herding, skijoring and therapy. Because the committee suspected that Samoyeds were doing work that the committee did not know about or had not even contemplated, they added a Special Application category for those unusual Samoyeds. The degrees were Working Samoyed (WS) 1000 points, and Working Samoyed Excellent (WSX) 1500 points.

Once the programme was established in 1991, interest in working with Samoyeds seemed to swell daily. People from all over the country began to earn their points and submit their documentation. By 1998 over 150 working degrees had been awarded and a new category, Master Working Samoyed (WSXM requiring 5000 points) had been added. The committee had awarded special application points for dogs that had performed in movies, hauled rocks and logs off trails, worked as service dogs for the wheelchair-bound, and run in skijor races. For those unfamiliar with the work involved in each of the categories, a short description follows.

RACE AND EXCURSION
SLEDDING AND CARTING
Samoyed sled and carting teams, are now hitting the trails from one end of the country to the other. As many as nine Samoyed teams were competing in races in the Colorado Rockies during 1998. On the east coast, one dedicated Sammy musher has started her own school for novice dog drivers. In the far northwest and in areas of the country with less snow, the sled runners are exchanged for wheeled carts. The best way to learn the skill is to go out with experienced team drivers, go to sled races, and ask many

Donna Dannen race sledding at the Frisco Gold Mush.

Donna and Kribou hauling out cut trees for a Forestry management project.

questions. A couple of good books on the basics are *Mush* from the Sierra Nevada Dog Drivers, or Lee Fishback's *Training Novice Sled Dogs*, available from mushing supply catalogues.

Once a beginner knows something about how intensively he or she wants to take part in this sport, the dogs will need to be trained so that each knows what is expected of it. This can be done by working with each dog individually while the budding driver jogs or bikes along. Above all, it is necessary to be sure the dogs are having fun. If they are not having fun, they will make a poor team.

Necessary basic equipment includes a sled and gangline with tuglines for each dog, harnesses, snowhook (to anchor the sled when stopped), snub line with a quick release snap (for holding the sled while the dogs are hooked up) and a tie-out line for before and after a race, or when camping out.

For Sammy owners who would rather just enjoy the trails and the dogs than compete with them, the SCA Working Committee created the excursion category. Dogs can earn points by pulling the sleds or carts 10 miles or more (five miles for a two-dog team) if their owners will document the experience with pictures, maps and narrative.

SKIJORING

For those who only have one or two Samoyeds, skijoring is a good alternative for race or excursion sledding. Skijoring is a Norwegian term describing a person on skis being pulled by a horse or a vehicle or by a dog or dogs. All it requires is a dog, a sledding harness, a skijor belt and line, and skis to go sailing down the snowy trails behind an excited Samoyed. Some people take their ski poles for added balance. In northern Europe, skijoring is a major competitive sport in which the dog pulls a light sled while the human skis along.

In the United States, skijoring began as a non-competitive recreation, and remains so for most enthusiasts. In the last few years, however, dog sled races have added skijoring events to their schedules; it is fast becoming popular as a competitive event. Though the sport sounds simple, the human component of the pair should be an able cross-country skier. The dogs can become discouraged if they must continually stop to wait while their human drags him or herself up out of the snow.

49

Roger Landers skijoring on the Paul Bunyon trail in Minnesota.

Training the dog to pull a person on skis is no different from sled training. The same commands apply (gee – right, haw – left, let's go, and whoa are the basics) and the same techniques can be used to train individual dogs. Keep the training positive and praise lavishly when the dog does something right.

WEIGHT PULL
Weight pull is a safe, fun event in which dogs compete to determine which can pull the heaviest load a short distance in the least time. The International Weight Pull Association (IWPA) sanctions pulls

Chinook's Trek T'Saratoga at a Colorado.

in the United States and Europe that are organised by local clubs. Under the IWPA rules, a dog has 60 seconds to pull a wheeled cart or snow sledge a total of 16 feet. If the dog succeeds, he can advance to the next round in which more weight is added to the cart. The dog continues to compete until he fails to make the pull within the 60 second limit. Dogs are entered in weight classes; each dog competes against other dogs (of many breeds) within its own weight division. Again, it is crucial that the dog have fun in this competition, or he certainly is not going to pull. Keep the training exciting.

Basic equipment for this event is a well-padded weight pull harness. Dogs should not be pulling seriously until they are at least 18 to 24 months old, with fully developed skeletal and muscle structure. However, younger dogs (even puppies) can get used to wearing a harness and dragging a light stick around so they become familiar with something following along behind them making noise. Good conditioning is imperative for this sport, as it is for all the others. This can be achieved by simple roadwork – two miles a day three to four times a week. Sometimes the dogs can run in harness dragging a small log or tire (such as a boat-trailer tire) behind them. Once the dog understands the weight-pull procedure, spend more time on conditioning than weight-pull training.

PACK HIKING
Sammies seem to take to pack hiking eagerly with very little introduction. For thousands of years, on almost all continents, dogs have been carrying their humans' belongings. Nowadays the cordura pack has replaced the old leather

Roger Landers pack hiking in the Medicine Bow Mountains.

bags, but otherwise the experience is the same. Pack hiking allows many options. Hikers can set their own schedule, go alone or with a group, pick their favourite places, go around the park or up the mountain, make it easy or difficult, long or short, a day or afternoon hike or a three-week trek. In order to accumulate 25 points, the SCA requires that a dog carry 25 per cent of its weight a minimum of five miles. These hikes must be documented with pictures, maps and comments, as well as a listing of the pack contents and weights of both dog and pack items. Dogs and companions can work up to this by carrying lighter weights for two- to three-mile hikes near home until both are ready for something more.

Packs are the basic equipment needed; these can be purchased from most good dog outfitters. Some packs have a saddle that holds the bags on with velcro so that the packs can be removed for lunch or

rest stops without unstrapping everything. Dogs should always be on lead when pack hiking. Other basic necessities include water bottles (dogs will need a lot of water – up to four pints for a ten-mile hike) and bootees for sore or injured feet. Keep the load balanced by packing several small items instead of a few large ones. The human contingent should wear hiking boots, and a hat with a brim; it's wise to carry a rain jacket, a warm layer, lunch, compass, maps, small knife, extra plastic bags and sun screen.

HERDING

Originally the Samoyed Club of America Working Dog Program awarded points to dogs that competed in herding trials offered by clubs such as the American Herding Breeds Association. Later, the American Kennel Club instituted its own herding trial competition, so the SCA working program deferred to the AKC awards. Samoyeds successfully petitioned to be allowed to compete in these trials, because of their reindeer herding heritage, even though they were part of the AKC working (not herding) group. Now Samoyeds take part in herding training and seminars all over the country. A small but growing number have actually competed and earned herding titles.

The best way to start learning about herding is to participate in a seminar or in a herding instinct test. In the United States these are held by many different stock dog clubs, both local and national. At the seminar or instinct test the dog and owner will have the opportunity to be in the arena with the stock (usually sheep, although ducks are sometimes used). The trainer will work with the dog and owner to assess the dog's

Barbara Page's Vanilla Fudge learning to herd sheep.

reaction to the sheep. It is exciting to watch a dog that has never seen sheep before suddenly discover its sleeping instinct and begin to round them up. The moment of awakening is often clearly discernible.

If the dog possesses a good herding instinct and the owner wants to pursue further training, there are people who have land and sheep who will provide that training. A good instructor has trained a number of stock dogs; he or she can teach people how to work with their own dogs and learn to read the reactions of the livestock. Again, it is imperative that the training be kept positive, and that the dog and owner are physically fit and in good health. A good sense of humour is another asset for owners. Equipment is minimal; all that is needed is a good buckle collar and perhaps a shepherd's crook.

THERAPY
Pet-assisted therapy takes advantage of the Samoyed's most obvious charms and uses them to create human smiles. It is the one thing Sammies do that benefits others more than their owners. Samoyeds, being the people-loving dogs that they are, are a natural for therapy work in hospitals and nursing homes. In addition, their beautiful coats draw the eyes of the patients and make them less

threatening than other dogs of their size. Several organisations in the United States certify dogs for therapy work. They require that the dogs should be outgoing and friendly and have some very basic obedience training. In addition they need to be clean and have received all their vaccinations.

Hospitals, nursing homes, paediatric care facilities, and schools for the handicapped are all looking for such visits. Some are taking the therapy a step further by using dogs in physical therapy to retrieve balls, tug against a patient's pull or help with walkers or wheelchairs. Some special Samoyeds are actually working as service-dogs for the wheelchair-bound, performing such tasks as pulling the chair, opening doors, picking out groceries from the shelves, taking money to the cashier and bringing back change. One such Samoyed knows and responds to 85 separate commands. Becoming involved in therapy work is extremely rewarding. It allows Samoyed owners to witness the little miracles, like winning a smile from a severely ill child, that take place during therapy visits.

Nancy Stitley's Ch. Whytekrest's Sunny Spirit CD TDI, visiting Pitman Manor nursing home.

ENCOURAGING PEOPLE TO WORK THEIR SAMS

Interest in encouraging people to work with their dogs has grown both within and outside of the SCA. As the numbers of titled dogs has increased, the SCA has added a class at the Annual National Specialty Show that is limited to dogs with working titles. At the 1998 show the winner of the working bitch class went on to Best of Opposite Sex. Actual performance events at the National Specialty have also grown to include herding trials, weight pull, agility, and sometimes even an organised pack hike and a therapy dog evaluation. The club has added a lifetime Reward of Merit (ROM) that can be achieved by demonstrating outstanding working ability.

Outside the SCA, the Organisation for Working Samoyeds now includes top awards not only for sledding but also for skijoring, herding, obedience, and agility achievements. In 1998 for the first time the American Kennel Club sanctioned a show for both conformation and working titled dogs, called the Field of Champions Exposition. The only dogs that were eligible had to have both a conformation Championship and a working title either from the AKC or from the parent breed club if the club was a member of the AKC.

Samoyeds were allowed to participate if they had either an AKC herding title or an SCA working title. Five Samoyed Champions participated in this first show of its kind. Best of Breed went to Champion Tundra Winds' Talkeetna Tuktu WS who also was Best of Winners at the Samoyed Club of America National Specialty just two months previously.

WHY WORK WITH SAMOYEDS?

In the spring of 1998 I asked some owners of working Sams to tell me what they learned about their dogs, both mentally and physically, in the course of that work. Their answers were intriguing.

STRUCTURE AND MOVEMENT

Several told me that working the dogs provides insight into why good structure is so vital. The work tells us which dogs have endurance, strength and perseverance. It shows us the importance of good feet, senses, tails and toplines in accomplishing tasks, and it shows us how structure translates to efficiency of movement, endurance, and working attitude. Poor structure translates to choppy running which leads to early exhaustion and joints that must hurt. Dogs that hurt will not run. Badly structured rears seem to have less impact on the ability to run distances than faulty fronts.

WORK AND THE SAMMY MIND

As compelling and useful as the insights into structure and movement are, what is truly intriguing is the glimpse permitted into the dogs' minds and souls. It is the best opportunity to learn about each one as an individual. One learns what they like, what they do not like, what motivates them, whether they have a work ethic. Work seems to be important to the dogs. They often love to do the work, demonstrating this by their excitement when the harness or pack is brought out and by their enthusiasm on the trail once they have started. Owners have observed happier, stronger and healthier dogs since they started working. The dogs seem to thrive on challenges.

One driver of a team says: "I am amazed how they pick up on what we want to do and really seem to enjoy working together as a unit. In the kennels they have their own pecking order, but show them a harness and soon the pack turns into a team in which they all know their places and what is expected of them." Another observed that "not only their muscles, but their overall attitude improves."

LEARNING TO COMMUNICATE

One owner said one of the most important things she learns when she works with her dogs is how to be a better trainer, how to get the most from her dogs. In herding training she learns about her dog's natural drives and how to mould those so they benefit her not only in herding, but in everyday living. She uses the dog's own drives and needs in order to achieve a better recall or better behaviour around the house.

THE EMOTIONAL BOND

Above all, however, those who work with their dogs dwelled on the relationship, the bond that is created between canine and human, two different species, who strive together for a common purpose. A very special relationship develops between trainer and dog that grows with each activity and with the amount of time spent in that activity. The more the work, the deeper the relationships. In the final reckoning, working with the dogs is just as good for the human soul as for the canine, as several people said with great feeling.

"We have seen the beauty and strength of Samoyeds in harness running across a snowy field," say Corey and Christine Kreif. "We have discovered wonderful things about our beloved working companions." For all the Samoyeds' open, friendly and enthusiastic approach to life, however, and despite all we can learn about them when we work with them as team-mates, they still keep some secrets. "The more I know the more I realise how little I know about them," Helen Smith says. I am convinced that there remains something elusive in their minds and hearts, perhaps related to the wild land of ice and snow from which they come, that will always remain a tantalising mystery worth a lifetime to explore.

Zakinthos My Dream Girl Del Corno Bianco, an Agility competitor based in Italy. Samoyed owners agree that they develop a better relationship by working with their dogs.

The adaptable Samoyed enjoys all types of different activities. This group is owned by Ros Reynolds-Parnham.

THE SAMOYED IN THE UK

Ken Warburton of Cheshire raced his Samoyed, Rudi, in the early days of sled-dog racing being promoted in the UK. Sometimes he was the only Samoyed competitor. He has appeared on TV racing his dogs, while the whole Warburton family, including wife Rosemary and their daughters, have been pictured in magazines and been interviewed for radio. Ken is also much in demand as an after-dinner speaker on sled dog racing.

David Cox and his wife Sheila, of Oxford, have the impressive distinction of being the owners of the only racing Samoyed to win Best of Breed at Crufts.

Both Ken and Dave agree that a delightful experience is to be gained by working their Samoyeds. It is, after all, a type of work for which the breed was used and the dogs themselves obviously love it.

The British Sled Dog Championships are open to all pure-bred Siberian Huskies, Alaskan Malamutes, Eskimo Dogs and Samoyeds. The sport is soon to be recognised by the International Olympic Committee, so, eventually, contenders will be seen competing in the Winter Olympics. The Annual Series consists of six Championship races, three in England and three in Scotland with a warm-up event. A brochure for the British Sled Dog Racing Championships can be obtained from The Stables, Old Park Ride, Waltham Cross, Herts. EN7 5HY. Also available via the Internet: http://www.sleddog.com

ADAPTING TO UK CONDITIONS
By Ken Warburton

It is my belief that Samoyeds in this country are seen mainly at dog shows. With a few notable exceptions, I think little has been done to promote the working character of the breed. Throughout the world, the Samoyed was originally defined as being in the Working Group, although since 1999 it has been placed in the Pastoral (herding) Group in the UK. The breed should be capable of working in the very real sense of the word. Indeed, the Breed Standard contains the description "capable of great endurance".

When the breed was first introduced into the British Isles there was little, if any, true working of the Spitz Breeds. Since Samoyeds were mostly exhibited at shows, I personally feel that over a number of years this has caused vast changes within the breed. So many Samoyed look beautiful in the ring – but

Ken Warburton racing his Samoyed alongside two Siberian Huskies.

too much emphasis is placed on a pleasing outline. When it comes to movement, it is obvious that many of them would not survive long as working dogs in a working environment. I find that the drive from the rear has disappeared and that some bone formation is becoming too fine. Many of the dogs are lacking in muscle, and without muscle they will not have drive. Without drive, they cannot work properly. Let us consider what is meant by the expression "a working Samoyed". This term could be used to cover a number of activities:

Trekking
Dogs in harness, walking at normal speed but covering long distances.

Dog orienteering
Walking with back packs placed on either side of the dog's back.

Working and racing
Competing in teams using either a sled or wheeled rig.

Herding
In their original environment in Russia Samoyeds were used extensively as

herding dogs. There are no similar activities in the UK, only in the USA.

Let us now take a more detailed look at what would be considered as the main working activities carried out in the UK.

BACK PACKING AND MOUNTAIN RESCUE WORK
A number of Samoyed have been used for mountain rescue work in the mountains of North Wales. Noel Hulmston was a co-founder of the Clwyd Mountain Rescue Team. During visits to Alaska, Sweden and Norway he came across a number of dogs being used in rescue work in those countries where they pulled sleds on which there were medical supplies or injured persons. Noel purchased four Samoyeds, training them to work in harness and pull sleds. When the helicopters were grounded, the dog sled team could still operate.

SLED DOG RACING
This basically means taking a team of dogs in harness, pulling a sled or wheeled rig over a defined trail against the clock on a time-trial basis. In the UK much of the winter, although cold, is without snow. Accordingly, the sport had to be modified to take account of this. In these dry conditions, a wheeled rig, incorporating braking and steering systems, is used instead of a sled. The rigs, sleds, harnesses and tow lines are subject to strict rules. It is vitally important that the correct harness and lines are used. An ill-fitting harness can ruin a dog for life, making him refuse to work. It is essential to get an individual harness for each dog, in order to make all the strain and pressure rest upon the shoulders and chest.

Pressure should never be permitted on the throat or back and there should be maximum freedom both to forelegs and to hindquarters. All harnesses and lines have been developed on ideas from Alaska with individual improvements made. The main criterion is to have good, well-trained dogs. However, when good dogs are in harness, even with a team of 'naturals', it is necessary to put in a great deal of time, hard work and effort in order to train them properly.

There is always something new to learn. Training comes as no hardship to a true 'musher' (driver) who enjoys his dogs. It is continually rewarding to learn the individual characteristics of each dog.

It was in the 1970s that sled dog racing was started in Europe, possibly having been introduced by American servicemen. At this time the first Siberian Huskies were imported from America by the Fostal family, with the intention of introducing working sled dogs to the UK. A first rally was held near London.

By 1979, a second rally was staged at Cannock Chase, Staffordshire, when Chris and Ian McRae, who mainly owned Samoyeds, took part with their three Samoyeds and one Siberian husky. These then were the first Samoyeds to race in harness in the UK.

For several years they were the mainstay of the Samoyed world, promoting and enhancing their reputation in sled dog racing. During the 1980s, I introduced a duo of a Samoyed and a Siberian Husky into a mixed sled dog class. For three years they worked together in harness very successfully. Although Siberian Huskies are undoubtedly much quicker in harness, even the staunchest supporter has to admit that there was no finer sight than that of a Samoyed finishing a race, especially in the snow, pulling for all his worth and all the time enjoying it because he was always laughing and smiling. Eventually, however, the duo became unbalanced as the dogs matured. The Husky got quicker while the Samoyed stayed at a steady pace. This meant, by nature of his gait, that the Husky was doing all the work, which was a little unfair, and Rudi, my Samoyed was retired.

Working with a full team of Samoyeds alleviates that problem, since the gait and movement of a Samoyed is vastly different to a Siberian Husky, but other problems can occur. From a musher's point of view, it is more difficult to work Samoyeds in harness in comparison with other sled dogs. This is because of their independence and stubborn streak. It is fairly true to say that Samoyeds appear only to want to work if and when they feel like it. I feel more emphasis should be placed on breeding and training dispositions.

Another problem to be overcome is the 'balling up' of snow on the feet when running in the snow. With all the long coat and featherings, there is a tendency to ice up, leading to great difficulty in walking, let alone running. I would recommend that, while the dog is in harness or on snow, the wool on the feet be clipped short and treated with some form of grease to alleviate the problem. Other sled dogs, because of their shorter coat, do not experience this difficulty. The length of coat itself can be a big disadvantage, there being quite a lot of work involved in keeping dogs clean and the coat free of tangles. Again, this is not a trait found in other, shorter-coated sled dogs.

Dave Cox racing his Samoyeds in Scotland.

RUNNING A SAMOYED TEAM
By Dave Cox

The current scene is looking very good, with more and more people joining the sled dog events. We use a three-wheel rig because of the lack of snow, and the sledding season runs from the end of September through to March, taking place on frequent weekends in various parts of the country. Many events take place on Forestry Commission land or private parkland. Although Samoyed teams do run in these events, I feel we could do more, since it is the breed with least representation. Most teams run in the two-dog class, running about three miles. The four and six dog teams run about five miles. Distance is up to the organiser. If conditions are good, distance can be lengthened. Teams normally set off at two-minute intervals and race against the clock, the fastest time being the winner of that class. Marshalls are placed around the course to ensure that there is fair play by all participants and also to help a team if necessary.

The 1999 Siberian Husky Club event at Aviemore in Scotland was well attended. Seven all-Samoyed teams took part. This was two less than the previous year, due to bitches in whelp and one team having the misfortune of having three bitches in heat at the same time. Additionally, however, there were individual Samoyeds racing in mixed teams. When I am out training my dogs, I am often approached by other Samoyed owners who are convinced that their dogs would be good in harness, advising me that they pull in exercising. That is indeed true, but my advice is that the dogs must be built up and brought along steadily, much like an athlete in training.

When considering coming into the sport, it is wise to gain as much information as possible. If you are keen and willing to listen, most people in the sport will gladly help you get started. Second-hand rigs do become available at the end of the season and most of the other equipment required to run dogs in harness is made by a small band of mushers.

To get the season under way, the Siberian Husky Club runs a beginners Teach-In at Cannock Chase. Since the Siberian Husky Club and the Affiliated British Sleddog Activities are the two main organisations, it is necessary for anyone wishing to participate to go through these bodies. This ensures that a check is made on every dog expected to run – that it is the right age, meaning over twelve months, that it is a qualifying breed and also to ensure that dogs are not ill-treated at any time during a meeting.

When running a sled team, it is a thrill to see just how much the dogs enjoy it. Our own dogs get so excited, that it is really hard to hold them back. At the race meeting, the dogs are put out on the stake chain line, waiting for their turn to run. Sometimes, when dogs are running, they can sustain injury. Mostly this is cut pads or blisters. A precaution like putting bootees on the feet eliminates this problem. I do find that the biggest injury to our dogs is the injury to their pride.

When, after a run in the forest, they are wet, muddy and plastered from head to toe in mud, they certainly need a dog bath to make them presentable again. Most Samoyed owners who run their dogs also show them. Although all our dogs enjoy running, it is difficult to get a dog to run out in front as a lead dog. A dog can be put in a lead position and it will move forward, but will not like it, unless it has something to chase. It is important, therefore, to find one who just loves to run out in front. Since Samoyeds are not that fast compared to Siberian Huskies, they are known as a freighting breed, which means that they are used to pulling loads over longer distances but more slowly.

One of the biggest problems during the summer months, is keeping the dogs well exercised and fit to pull. To do this, it is necessary to get up at the crack of dawn in order to run the dogs in the coolest part of the day before the sun gets up. As can be appreciated, a heavily-coated Samoyed could soon become hot and overheat, and that could prove fatal to the dog. On nice summer days, the dogs run or train on the downs and we have breakfast before setting off back home. We find that if we feed the dogs twice a day, half in the morning and half at night, they do work better. During the non-working season, they are fed on low-protein food which helps keep their weight down. During the working season they will move onto a high-protein food.

OBEDIENCE TRAINING
There are so many ways our lovely breed can be worked and enjoyed. One of these is the field of Obedience training. Harold Bellamy and his first wife Joyce were well known for working their Samoyeds and as a result one of their dogs appeared in Dr. Findlay's casebook on TV. They were not alone; Carol and Jim Walker appeared on a TV Show, *That's my dog*. Their Samoyed did a scent exercise and won £286 for charity. Currently Norma Richardson of Manchester and Helen Black of Aberdeen are known as eager participants. Helen in particular manages to combine the role of showing and Obedience work with three-year-old Snowmyth Sno Secret To Kanyak, known as Nico.

OBEDIENCE COMPETITION
by Helen Black
Obedience with any breed is fun, but with a Samoyed it brings fun, laughter, tears of frustration, success and often disappointment because you know they can do it when they want to, so you must have a good sense of humour. The benefits of Obedience training are numerous. An

A ten-strong Samoyed team in Sweden.

obedient dog is not only a joy to its owner but also to other people and their dogs; that is why many owners attend classes – and also the reason I began. There are seven exercises for Obedience Competition.

1 HEELWORK
2 RECALL
3 RETRIEVE
4 DISTANCE CONTROL
5 SEND AWAY
6 SCENT DISCRIMINATION
7 STAY (Two-minute sit-stay. Ten-minute down-stay)

I have been doing Obedience with Nico for just about two years and have successfully achieved five of the seven exercises to a high standard. At the moment we are concentrating on scent work, which is hard, due to the concentration required, and our next and last exercise will be distance control. This can be done in one of two ways, either by giving commands orally or by hand signals. The first year of Nico's life was spent in the show ring so, when we took him to classes, he did not even know the meaning of the word "sit", which brought lots of laughter from the other members of the class; but now, two years later, I am as proud as punch when he is used by the trainer to show new members the speed and accuracy required for the above exercises.

Obedience develops a close bond between dog and handler as the dogs are always alert awaiting the next command. If you have ever watched any breed compete in Obedience, you will see how much they

Helen Black with 'Nico' who competes in Obedience.

enjoy it, but no dog can be forced – it must be made to understand in a firm manner. Samoyeds love to be involved in any activity with human companions and with Obedience the better they do the more praise they get, the better they compete. Even if you never intend to compete and do it only to make your dog more sociable, you will be amazed at how well they can do and how much fun it can be for both of you It is, I am sure, preferable to hours of boredom in the house. There is a bonus, too, with Obedience, since a Samoyed can be worked out of coat. It just goes to prove that not only does our breed have beauty but brains as well.

6 THE BREED STANDARDS

The Breed Standard is the specification of the Breed. It is the Standard by which dogs are judged in the showring. The object of the written Standard is to create a picture of a Samoyed. Inevitably it will be interpreted differently by individuals.

THE UK SAMOYED STANDARD
(Reprinted by kind permission of The Kennel Club)

GENERAL APPEARANCE Most striking, of medium size and well-balanced, strong, active and graceful, free from coarseness but capable of great endurance.

CHARACTERISTICS Intelligent, alert, full of action, "smiling expression".

TEMPERAMENT Displays affection to all mankind. Unprovoked nervousness or aggression highly undesirable.

HEAD AND SKULL Head powerful, wedge-shaped, with broad, flat skull, muzzle medium length, tapering foreface not too sharply defined. Lips black. Hair short and smooth before ears. Nose black for preference, but may be brown or flesh-coloured.

EYES Almond-shaped, set slanted, medium to dark brown, set well apart when alert, intelligent expression. Eye-rims unbroken black. Light or black eyes undesirable.

EARS Thick, not too long, slightly rounded at tips, set well apart and well covered with inside hair. Fully erect in adults.

MOUTH Jaws strong with a perfect, regular and complete scissor bite, i.e. 0upper teeth closely overlapping the lower teeth and set square to the jaws.

NECK Strong, not too short, and proudly arched.

FOREQUARTERS Shoulders well laid, legs muscular with good bone and not too short.

HINDQUARTERS Very muscular, stifles well angulated, viewed from the rear, legs straight and parallel, with well let down hocks. Cow hocks or straight stifles highly undesirable.

BODY Back medium in length, broad and muscular with exceptionally strong loin. Chest deep but not too broad, well sprung ribs, giving plenty of heart and lung room.

The Samoyed in Britain: Ch. Zamoyski Lucky Claudia.

FEET Long, flattish, slightly spread and well feathered. Round cat-feet undesirable.

TAIL Long, profusely coated, carried over the back and to side when alert, sometimes dropped when at rest.

GAIT/MOVEMENT Moves freely with strong agile drive, showing power and elegance.

COAT Body should be well covered with thick, close, soft and short undercoat, with harsh but wiry hair growing through it, forming weather-resistant outer coat which should stand away from the body and be free from curl.

COLOUR Pure white, white and biscuit, cream, outer coat silver-tipped.

SIZE Dogs 51-56cm (20-22ins) at shoulder. Bitches 46-51cm (18-20ins) at shoulder. Weight in proportion to size.

FAULTS Any departure from the foregoing points should be considered a fault and the seriousness with which the fault should be regarded should be in exact proportion to its degree.

Note: male animals should have two apparently normal testicles fully descended into the scrotum.

OFFICIAL AKC STANDARD FOR THE SAMOYED APPROVED 1993
(Reprinted by kind permission of the American Kennel Club)

GENERAL CONFORMATION

(a) General Appearance – The Samoyed, being essentially a working dog, should present a picture of beauty, alertness and strength, with agility, dignity and grace.
As his work lies in cold climates, his coat should be heavy and weather-resistant, well-groomed, and of good quality rather than quantity. The male carries more of a "ruff" than the female. He should not be long in back, as a weak back would make him practically useless for his legitimate work, but at the same time, a close-coupled body would also place him at a great disadvantage as a draft dog. Breeders should aim for the happy medium, a body not long but muscular, allowing liberty, with a deep chest and well-sprung ribs, strong neck, straight front and especially strong loins. Males should be masculine in appearance and deportment without unwarranted aggressiveness; bitches feminine without weakness of structure or apparent softness of temperament. Bitches may be slightly longer in back than males. They should both give the appearance of being capable of great endurance but be free from coarseness. Because of the depth of chest required, the legs should be moderately long. A very short-legged dog is to be deprecated. Hindquarters should be particularly well-developed, stifles well-bent and any suggestion of unsound stifles or cowhocks severely

The Samoyed in North America:
Ch. Sanorka's Moonlight Trip T' Ren J.

penalized. General appearance should include movement and general conformation, indicating balance and good substance.

(b) Substance – Substance is that sufficiency of bone and muscle which rounds out a balance with the frame. The bone is heavier than would be expected in a dog of this size but not so massive as to prevent the speed and agility most desirable in a Samoyed. In all builds, bone should be in proportion to body size. The Samoyed should never be so heavy as to appear clumsy nor so light as to appear racy. The weight should be in proportion to the height.

(c) Height – Males, 21 to 23½ inches; Females, 19 to 21 inches at the withers. An oversized or undersized Samoyed is to be penalized according to the extent of the deviation.

(d) Coat – (Texture and Condition) The Samoyed is a double-coated dog. The body should be well-covered with an undercoat of soft, short, thick close wool with longer and harsh hair growing through it to form the outer coat, which stands straight out from the body and should be free from curl. The coat should

form a ruff around the neck and shoulders, framing the head (more on males than on females). Quality of coat should be weather-resistant and considered more than quantity. A droopy coat is undesirable. The coat should glisten with a silver sheen. The female does not usually carry as long a coat as most males and it is softer in texture.

(e) Color – Samoyeds should be pure white, white and biscuit, cream, or all biscuit. Any other colors disqualify.

MOVEMENT

(a) Gait – The Samoyed should trot, not pace. He should move with a quick agile stride that is well-timed. The gait should be free, balanced and vigorous, with good reach in the forequarters and good driving power in the hindquarters. When trotting, there should be a strong rear-action drive. Moving at a slow walk or trot, they will not single track, but as speed increases, the legs gradually angle inward until the pads are finally falling on a line directly under the longitudinal center of the body. As the pad marks converge the forelegs and hind legs are carried straight forward in traveling, the stifles not turned in nor out. The back should remain strong, firm and level. A choppy or stilted gait should be penalized.

(b) Rear End – Upper thighs should be well-developed. Stifles well bent-approximately 45 degrees to the ground. Hocks should be well developed, sharply defined and set at approximately 30 percent of hip height. The hind legs should be parallel when viewed from the rear in a natural stance, strong, well-developed, turning neither in nor out. Straight stifles are objectionable. Double-jointedness or cowhocks are a fault. Cowhocks should only be determined if the dog has had an opportunity to move properly.

(c) Front End – Legs should be parallel and straight to the pasterns. The pasterns should be strong, sturdy and straight, but flexible with some spring for proper let-down of feet. Because of depth of chest, legs should be moderately long. Length of leg from the ground to the elbow should be approximately 55 percent of the total height at the withers – a very short-legged dog is to be deprecated. Shoulders should be long and sloping, with a layback of 45 degrees and be firmly set. Out at the shoulders or out at the elbows should be penalized. The withers separation should be approximately 1 to 1½ inches.

(d) Feet – Large, long, flattish; a hare foot, slightly spread but not splayed; toes arched; pads thick and tough, with protective growth of hair between the toes. Feet should turn neither in nor out in a natural stance but may turn in slightly in the act of pulling. Turning out, pigeon-toed, round or cat-footed or splayed are faults. Feathers on feet are not too essential but are more profuse on females than on males.

HEAD

(a) Conformation – Skull is wedge-shaped, broad, slightly crowned, not round or apple-headed, and should form an equilateral triangle on lines between the inner base of the ears and the center point of the stop.
Muzzle – Muzzle of medium length and medium width, neither coarse nor snipy;should taper toward the nose and be in proportion to the size of the dog and the width of the skull. The muzzle must have depth. Whiskers are not to be removed. Stop not too abrupt, nevertheless well defined.

Lips – Should be black for preference and slightly curved up at the corners of the mouth, giving the "Samoyed smile". Lip lines should not have the appearance of being coarse nor

should the flews drop predominately at corners of the mouth.

Ears – Strong and thick, erect, triangular and slightly rounded at the tips; should not be large or pointed, nor should they be small and "bear-eared". Ears should conform to head size and the size of the dog; they should be set well apart but be within the border of the outer edge of the head; they should be mobile and well covered inside with hair; hair full and stand-off before the ears. Length of ear should be the same measurement as the distance from inner base of ear to outer corner of eye.

Eyes – Should be dark for preference; should be placed well apart and deep-set; almond-shaped with lower lid slanting towards an imaginary point approximating the base of ears. Dark eye rims for preference. Round or protruding eyes penalized. Blue eyes disqualifying.

Nose – Black for preference but brown, liver, or Dudley nose not penalized. Color of nose sometimes changes with age and weather.

Jaws and Teeth – Strong, well-set teeth, snugly overlapping with scissors bite. Undershot or overshot should be penalized.

(b) Expression – The expression, referred to as "Samoyed expression", is very important and is indicated by sparkle of the eyes, animation and lighting up of the face when alert or intent on anything. Expression is made up of a combination of eyes, ears and mouth. The ears should be erect when alert; the mouth should be slightly curved up at the corners to form the "Samoyed smile".

TORSO

(a) Neck – Strong, well-muscled, carried proudly erect, set on sloping shoulders to carry

head with dignity when at attention.
Neck should blend into shoulders with a
graceful arch.

(b) Chest – Should be deep, with ribs well-sprung out from the spine and flattened at the sides to allow proper movement of the shoulders and freedom for the front legs. Should not be barrel-chested. Perfect depth of chest approximates the point of elbows, and the deepest part of the chest should be back of the forelegs near the ninth rib. Heart and lung room are secured more by body depth than width.

(c) Loin and Back – The withers forms the highest part of the back. Loins strong and slightly arched. The back should be straight to the loin, medium in length, very muscular, and neither long nor short-coupled. The dog should be "just off square", the length being approximately 5 percent more than the height. Females allowed to be slightly longer than males. The belly should be well-shaped and tightly muscled and, with the rear of the thorax, should swing up in a pleasing curve (tuck-up). Croup must be full, slightly sloping, and must continue imperceptibly to the tail root.

(d) Tail – The tail should be moderately long with the tail bone terminating approximately at the hock when down. It should be profusely covered with long hair and carried forward over the back or side when alert, but sometimes dropped when at rest. It should not be high or low set and should be mobile and loose, not tight over the back. A double hook is a fault. A judge should see the tail over the back once when judging.

(e) Disposition – Intelligent, gentle, loyal, adaptable, alert, full of action, eager to serve, friendly but conservative, not distrustful or shy, not overly aggressive. Unprovoked aggressiveness to be severely penalized.

DISQUALIFICATIONS – Any color other than pure white, cream, biscuit, or white and biscuit. Blue eyes.

FCI STANDARD
No. 212 / 17.11.1997 / GB
(Reprinted by kind permission of the FCI)

SAMOYED

(Samoiedskaia Sabaka)

ORIGIN: Northern Russia and Siberia.
PATRONAGE: Nordic Countries / NKU.
DATE OF PUBLICATION OF THE
ORIGINAL VALID STANDARD: 22.07.1997

UTILIZATION: Sledge and companion dog.

CLASSIFICATION: FCI Group 5 Spitz and primitive types. Section 1.2 Nordic sledge dogs. Without working trial.

BRIEF HISTORICAL SUMMARY The name Samoyed derives from the Samoyed Tribes in Northern Russia and Siberia. In Southern parts of the area they used white, black and brown parti-coloured dogs as reindeer herders; in the northern parts the dogs were pure white, had a mild temperament and were used as hunting and sledge dogs. The Samoyeds dogs lived close to their owners, they even slept within the shelters and were used as heaters. The British zoologist Ernest Kilburn-Scott spent three months among Samoyed Tribes in 1889. Returning to England he brought with him a brown male puppy called Sabarka. Later he imported a cream-coloured bitch called Whitey Petchora from the western side of the Urals and a snow-white male called Musti from Siberia. These few dogs and those brought by the

The Samoyed judged under FCI regulations: Int. Dk. Ch. Kaissa's First Son Of Jonah.

explorers are the base for the western Samoyed. The first Standard was written in England in 1909.

GENERAL APPEARANCE Medium in size, elegant, a white Arctic Spitz. In appearance gives the impression of power, endurance, charm, suppleness, dignity and self-confidence. The expression, the so-called "Samoyed Smile", is made up of a combination of eye shape and position, and the slightly curved up corners of the mouth. The sex should be clearly stamped.

IMPORTANT PROPORTIONS The length of the body is approximately 5 per cent more than the height at the withers. The depth of the body is slightly less than the half of the height at the withers. The muzzle is approximately as long as the skull.

BEHAVIOUR AND TEMPERAMENT Friendly, open, alert and lively. The hunting instinct is very slight. Never shy nor aggressive. Very social and cannot be used as guard dog. **HEAD** Powerful and wedge-shaped.

CRANIAL REGION Viewed from the front and in profile only slightly convex. Broadest between the ears. Stop: Clearly defined but not too prominent. Slightly visible furrow between the eyes.

FACIAL REGION Nose: Well developed, preferably black. During some periods of the year the pigment of the nose can fade to a so-called "winter nose"; there must, however, always be dark pigment at the edges of the nose. Muzzle: Strong and deep, approximately as long as the skull, gradually tapering towards the nose, neither snipy nor heavy and square. The bridge of the nose is straight. Lips: Close fitting, black and rather full. The corners of the mouth are slightly curved forming the characteristic "Samoyed Smile". Jaws/Teeth/Bite: Regular and complete scissor bite. The teeth and the jaws are strong. Normal dentition. Eyes: Dark brown in colour, well-set in the sockets, placed rather apart, somewhat slanting and almond-shaped. The expression is "smiling", kind, alert and intelligent. The eye-rims are black. Ears: Erect, rather small, thick, triangular and slightly rounded at the tips. They should be mobile, set high; due to the broad skull, well apart.

NECK Strong and of medium length with a proud carriage.

BODY Slightly longer than the height at the withers, deep and compact but supple. Withers: Clearly defined. Back: Of medium length, muscular and straight; in females slightly longer than in males. Loin: Short, very strong and defined. Croup: Full, strong, muscular and slightly sloping. Chest: Broad, deep and long, reaching almost to the elbows. The ribs are well sprung. Underline: Moderate tuck-up.

TAIL Set rather high. When the dog is alert and in motion the tail is carried bent from the root forward over the back or side, but may be hanging at rest, then reaching to the hocks.

LIMBS

FOREQUARTERS General appearance: Well placed and muscular with strong bones. Viewed from the front, straight and parallel. Shoulder: Long, firm and sloping. Upper arm: Oblique and close to the body; approximately as long as the shoulder. Elbow: Close to the body. Carpus: Strong but supple. Metacarpus (Pastern): Slightly oblique. Feet: Oval with long toes, flexible and pointing straight forward. Toes arched and not too tightly knit. Elastic pads.

HINDQUARTERS General appearance: Viewed from behind straight and parallel with very strong muscles. Upper thigh: Of medium length, rather broad and muscular. Stifle: Well angulated. Hocks: Rather low and well angulated. Metatarsus: Short, strong, vertical and parallel. Feet: As front feet. The dewclaws should be removed.

GAIT: Powerful, free and tireless in appearance with long stride. Good reach in the forequarters and good driving power in the hindquarters.

COAT

HAIR Profuse, thick, flexible and dense polar coat. The Samoyed is double-coated dog with short, soft and dense undercoat and longer, more harsh and straight outer coat. The coat should form a ruff around the neck and shoulders framing the head, especially in males. On head and on front of legs, hair is short and smooth; on outside of ears short, standing off and smooth. Inside the ears should be well furred. On back of the thighs the hair forms trousers. There should be a protective growth of hair between the toes. The tail should be profusely covered with hair. The coat of the female is often shorter and softer in texture than that of the male. The correct coat texture should always have a special glistening sheen.

COLOUR: Pure white, cream or white with biscuit. (The basic colour to be white with a few biscuit markings.) Should never give the impression of being pale brown.

SIZE: Height at withers: Ideal height: male 57 cm with a tolerance of 3 cm, and females 53 cm with a tolerance of 3 cm.

FAULTS Any departure from the foregoing points should be considered a fault and the seriousness with which the fault should be regarded should be in exact proportion to its degree. Visible faults in structure. Light bone. Males not masculine and females not feminine. Pincer bite. Yellow eyes. Soft ears. Barrel ribcage. Double twisted tail. Low on the legs. Badly bow-legged or cow-hocked. Wavy or short-coated throughout; long, soft or coat hanging down. Aloofness.

SERIOUS FAULTS Clearly unpigmented areas on eye-rims or lips.

ELIMINATING FAULTS Eyes blue or of different colours. Overshot or undershot bite. Ears not erect. Coat colour other than permitted in the Standard. Shy or aggressive disposition.
NB Male animals should have two apparently normal testicles fully descended into the scrotum.

THE BREED STANDARDS DISCUSSED

Some years ago the Kennel Club altered the UK Breed Standard, which had been drawn up in 1909, in order to unify Standards with other breeds as much as possible. Although Breed Clubs were consulted, much detail was lost, particularly in the detailing of faults.

Close comparisons between the United Kingdom (UK), the American Kennel Club (AKC) and the Fédération Cynologique Internationale (FCI) Breed Standards throw up some considerable differences. Both the AKC and FCI Standards are much more acceptably detailed. The AKC Standard was amended in 1993, when the old Standard was considered inadequate and there were complaints of poor judging.

Attention must be given to these important differences when judging the breed in the respective countries, otherwise problems or complaints can occur. The FCI Standard covers the European and Scandinavian countries.

In the light of these differences, this is what I would require to see when judging, no matter where I was in the world.

General Appearance: I would bear in mind that the special characteristics of the breed have, in most part, been created by nature and are there to give protection to the animal.

Characteristics: "Smiling expression". It is interesting that in both the AKC and the FCI Standard the references to the Samoyed smile includes more detail. I consider this to be a unique feature of the breed. I would look for a wedge-shaped head combining a number of

The body should be long, not muscular. The male should be just off-square, the length being roughly 5 per cent more than the height. Bitches are allowed to be only slightly longer than males.

vital points. The tight black lips should curve slightly upwards at the corners of the mouth, showing no flews. Colour and eye shape are essential to the overall picture. The almond-shaped dark brown eyes should slant towards the base of the ears. The eye-rim should be totally black. From an open mouth a pink tongue should extend, showing a glimpse of pearly white teeth. A proudly arched neck should contribute to the happy picture of a Samoyed declaring – 'look at me!'.

Temperament: The temperament of most Samoyeds is superb. They love everybody and that is why they make such good pets. I would send out of the ring any Samoyed displaying open aggression.

Head and skull: On further examining the head, I would look for a 'roman' nose. I would be mindful that the UK Standard makes no reference to the fading that can occur. The AKC and FCI Standards explain that the Samoyed

68

nose can sometimes change colour due to age and weather, particularly in the winter months. The head should never appear narrow or snipy and, indeed, the AKC and FCI Standards make mention of the stop being defined. In the UK this could be why some 'dish faces' are sometimes allowed to creep in. Looking directly at the head, I would try to imagine snow falling at blizzard force. The shape of the head should ensure that the show would drift away to the side and up and over, thereby leaving the nose, ears and eyes clear to do their vital jobs. I would be aware that any exaggerated stop or 'dish face' would cause snow to collect at the top of the foreface and render the dog blind in its natural working conditions.

Eyes: These should be particularly beautiful, especially adding to the beauty of bitches. The strong eyelashes prevent falling or blowing snow from entering the eyes. Any bold, or hound-type eye would be utterly wrong in this head and would mean that the Samoyed would not be able to see in such a bright light as is found on the Arctic plains. The disqualification of blue eyes is referred to by both the AKC and FCI Standards and must be taken into account.

THE HEAD

Correct

Incorrect: Too coarse.

Incorrect: Too snipy.

Incorrect: Too wide.

69

THE EYES

THE EARS

Correct head and ear set.

Correct: Almond-shaped eyes, set slanted.

Incorrect ear shape.

Incorrect: ears set too wide.

Incorrect: Round eyes.

Incorrect: ears too long and too pointed.

FOREQUARTERS

Correct.   *Incorrect: too narrow.*   *Incorrect: Too wide.*   *Incorrect: Toeing in.*   *Incorrect: Toeing out.*   *Incorrect: Out at elbow.*

Ears: These are the Samoyed's most used tool – hearing the noises of the wild, the commands of their owner and the yapping of their kennel mates. If the ears do not conform to the Standards and, on examination, were found to be thinner and more highly placed on the head, they would most certainly become frost-bitten in Arctic conditions. In a mature Samoyed the coat can become so profuse that the ears can hardly be seen at all. Some Samoyeds do possess exceptionally sensitive hearing.

Neck: When examining the Samoyed I would look to see a longer neck, which allows for longer muscles which contribute to better movement.

These muscles tire less easily than short, heavy ones and help to shift the centre of gravity, or balance point, of the dog.

Forequarters: There is some variance in all three Standards here. I would be looking for moderate angulation with withers being one-and-a-half inches apart to a moderate shoulder lay. I do feel that the AKC Standard is right to be specific about withers. Although the FCI make a reference, there is no separation measurement. The UK Standard makes no reference.

Hindquarters: I would hope not to see straight stifles, as this would mean a stilted action and a great wasting of energy. Conversely, too much angulation would make a dog weak and vulnerable to any unexpected movement such as a slip on the ice. I would suggest that the hindquarter sections in the AKC and FCI Standards make it easier for judges to know what they should be looking for.

HINDQUARTERS

Correct hindquarters and rear action.

Incorrect: Too close.

Incorrect: Too wide.

Incorrect: Out at hocks.

Incorrect: Cow hocks.

Incorrect: Feet turned out.

Body: The natural function of the Samoyed was to herd reindeer. The body of the dog being judged must, therefore, be found to have a body suited to this purpose. Too much length would give weakness when moving over long distances for long stretches of time. A body that was too short would mean the Samoyed being unable to endure the task of running all day. A body of medium length, strong yet racy, is needed. A good depth of chest is required, since much heart and lung room are needed for the active dog. A barrel chest would encumber its activities, while a narrow chest would mean that the dog would be unable to absorb oxygen for long spells. I would feel for strength in the loin and would look for a definite tuck-up which must be carried to ensure freedom of movement when running at a high speed.

Mouth: The FCI Standard mentions normal dentition. A complete set of dentition comprises 42 teeth.

Feet: The ground which the Samoyed would make contact with in his native habitat would be hard and very cold. The feet, therefore, need to be resilient, well-cushioned with hair, and with hard sharp nails to grip the ice. These qualities give

THE BITE

All dogs should have 42 teeth. In the upper jaw there should be 6 incisors, 2 canines, 8 premolars and 4 molars. In the lower jaw there should be 6 incisors, 2 canines, 8 premolars and 6 molars. The Samoyed should have a scissor bite, i.e. the upper teeth closely overlapping the lower teeth, and set square to the jaw.

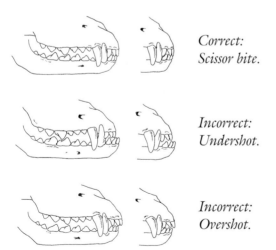

Correct: Scissor bite.

Incorrect: Undershot.

Incorrect: Overshot.

FEET

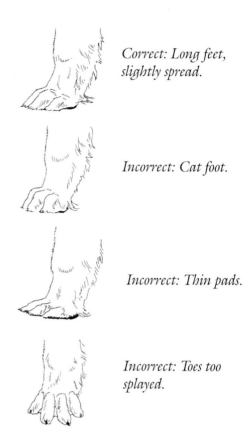

Correct: Long feet, slightly spread.

Incorrect: Cat foot.

Incorrect: Thin pads.

Incorrect: Toes too splayed.

the dog both protection and a safe base on which to stand.

Tail: It does not matter to which side of the Samoyed the tail curls. What is essential is that it does curl so that, when the dog is moving, the tail is carried over the back and away from the covering of snow on the ground. In the natural habitat, when asleep, the tail would curl around the dog's body, covering the nose and head to protect them from the snow, ice and Arctic winds. The AKC Standard makes reference to a double hook at the end of the tail, which is considered a

THE TAIL

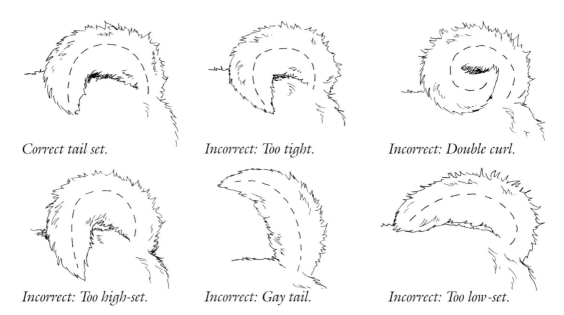

Correct tail set.

Incorrect: Too tight.

Incorrect: Double curl.

Incorrect: Too high-set.

Incorrect: Gay tail.

Incorrect: Too low-set.

fault. The FCI Standard also refers to a double twisted tail being a fault. I would always make allowances for a dropped tail on a very young puppy who might not yet be fully confident, provided that the tail was carried over the back while the dog was on the move.

Gait/Movement: A correctly moving Samoyed is a joy to behold. It should move so effortlessly that, when in full motion, it would seem that the dog's feet hardly touch the ground. The greater the speed in movement, the closer the feet will come into a centre line. A long, purposeful stride at the front should be followed by a purposeful drive behind, meaning that the dog should cover about twice the ground it stands on in one stride. A picture of almost single tracking will appear when the Samoyed is in full motion. A good maxim would be to say that the soundest dog moves with the least amount of effort. This section is

well detailed in the AKC Standard, and the FCI Standard also includes valuable points.

Coat: The AKC and the FCI Standards are practically identical in their references to the ruff, which I would always hope to see and do consider to be an important characteristic. Strangely, there is no reference to it in the UK Standard. Both the AKC and FCI Standards make reference to the difference in coat between a dog and a bitch. Although all the Standards mention the glistening, or silver sheen of the coat, I feel the AKC is correct to include all-biscuit as a colour. Dogs showing biscuit in their colour tend to have harsher coats and more dense pigmentation. In the best specimens, silver tips on the outer coat glisten like frost, especially when seen in sunlight or strong light. In Arctic conditions this would be necessary in order to resist the harsh glare of the sun.

A Samoyed with a correct type of coat will be resistant to rain and snow, with the top hairs protecting the dog from these elements. A soft, flowing coat, lacking in undercoat, or with too long outer hairs, will make the dog vulnerable to climatic conditions and will afford the body underneath no protection. In different countries it must be taken into account that coats can vary according to climate.

Size: When judging in the UK I would abide by the UK Standard of males 20 ins to 22 ins at shoulder (51 to 56 cms)

and females 18 ins to 20 ins (46 to 51 cms). Both the AKC and FCI Standards allow for bigger dogs and bitches. When judging under those Standards, their size criteria must be adhered to: US – males 21 ins to 23½ ins (53 to 59 cms) and females 19 ins to 21 ins (48 to 53 cms): FCI males 22½ ins. (57 cms) with 3 cms tolerance, females 21 ins (53 cms) with 3 cms tolerance.

The FCI Standard also makes reference to the removal of dewclaws and, in the UK, a spayed bitch or castrated dog can be shown if a medical certificate is obtained.

MOVEMENT

1. Correct movement viewed from the front.

2. Incorrect: Too wide, hackney action.

3. Incorrect: Too close.

Below: Correct action in profile. This is Can. Am. Ch. Vanderbilt's Krash Of Thunder CD, ADC, CCG.

7 *THE SHOW RING*

Many people feel that dog showing is an ideal hobby. There is certainly plenty of action and stimulation involved and it is a good way of making new friends who share a common interest.

WHY HAVE DOG SHOWS?

The whole idea of Dog Shows is deciding on the best exhibits. These, possibly, should then be bred from to ensure sound stock for the future. Be totally honest with yourself about your dog and try not to be blind to any glaring faults. If your dog really does not have potential, then you must accept this and enjoy the dog as a companion.

All dogs tend to vary in their condition and may not always be at their best on the day of the show. This could be due to a number of reasons, such as a health problem, just an 'off day', or a blowing coat. Blowing coats tend to be the main problem in the Samoyed breed. When a dog or bitch is at the peak of their condition and showing their best, it is not unusual for them to have a string of wins before factors change. In order to give your dog the very best opportunity,

it is up to you to prepare your dog through training and grooming to the best of your ability.

TRAINING FOR SHOWS

Remember, this is slightly different to Obedience, since the last thing you want is for your dog to sit down in the ring. It is not too difficult to train a young Samoyed puppy for the show ring. Start as early as you can at home, always making it fun and give plenty of praise. Teach your puppy to stand and walk. It is a good idea to use a meal as a motivator. For just a few seconds, hold the dish in front of the puppy and say "Stand". Lengthen the time each day. Get the puppy to move up and down the garden closely following the meal in your hand, and eventually attach the lead.

Try not to become repetitive or the puppy will become bored. When the puppy is three to four months old, look for your nearest ring training class. You should be able to obtain details from either your vet or the Secretary of any local Canine Society. At Ringcraft, the puppy will be exposed to plenty of barking dogs and noise. At first it will be

Dog and handler must work as a team. This is Roybridge Lucky Legacy with Donna Fleming.

a whole new world, but he will quickly get used to being handled by other people.

He will learn to stand still and get used to having his mouth examined for bite and check of pigmentation. It also is helpful if you can get friends to go over the puppy from time to time. Do bear in mind that Samoyeds are great extroverts and may embarrass you initially. I clearly remember my first Samoyed shattering a

glass pane in a door at the ringcraft class. I naively tied her to the door while I walked across the hall for a cup of tea. She tugged to come too, thus shaking the glass free.

In this breed it is acceptable to bait the dog, usually with small pieces of cooked liver which can be carried in a pocket or small pouch. This is used to attract the dog's attention, making the dog look alert when standing foursquare in front of you. To get the puppy acclimatised, enter for some small local shows before plunging into Championship shows. It is quite usual for a puppy to perform perfectly well at home but erratically in the show ring where there are other puppies and more distractions outside the ring, but do not be disheartened. I have often seen young puppies start off in the show ring behaving well but later playing up when they become blasé with the proceedings. It is a period some go through before settling down to show consistently.

PREPARATION FOR SHOW DAY

It is important to bath for every show no matter how small, or how important, that show is. It is easy to look at your dog and think that it is clean. Just wait until you arrive at the show and stand next to dogs that have been bathed – there is a marked difference. The ideal time to prepare for a show is three days beforehand.

To begin with it is essential to brush the dog thoroughly in order to get rid of dirt and dust and to brush out any tangles. Have everything ready and to hand for the bath. Wear as little as possible yourself. No matter how careful you are, you are bound to get wet. You will need to cover the bathroom floor with a sheet or similar and have to hand towels, cotton wool for ear plugs, shampoo, spray attachment or jug and a sponge. Any good dog shampoo can be used. It is also useful to place a non-slip rubber mat in the bath for your dog to stand on.

First, thoroughly wet the dog with lukewarm water using the spray attachment or bowl and jug. Ensure that the water is not too hot. Now add the shampoo and, using your fingers, rub

Pam Taylor showing Naduska Precious Panda. A lot of hard work goes into training a dog for exhibition. Photo: Carol Ann Johnson.

hard into the coat, working up a good lather. Pay particular attention to the areas around the ears, the front, inside the back legs, elbows, featherings and feet. Wash face and ears with a sponge, gently drying eyes with a towel to avoid soap. Rinse well and shampoo again if necessary. Do not forget to pay attention to the teeth, brushing if necessary. Squeeze excess water from the coat of the dog while still in the bath and absorb as much moisture as possible with a towel.

Remove the dog from the bath, placing him on the floor and allow him to shake. This is where you get really wet. Briskly towel the dog down using three or four towels. The dog will continue to shake and, once freed from the confinement of the bathroom, will dash about and enjoy rubbing himself along the carpet. Allow the dog outside to empty his bladder before placing on a grooming table for drying with a hand dryer. Place a towel on the table to again absorb moisture if you wish to lie the dog down. Brush and turn the dog as you dry with the hand dryer, covering all areas. It does take almost two full days for an adult Samoyed in full coat to become completely dry because the undercoat will retain moisture. At bedtime make sure the dog sleeps in a warm environment so that he does not get chilled.

The next day, groom your dog thoroughly as previously described and try and keep him clean until the show. This is in itself not always easy. After being bathed and groomed to perfection, one of my dogs once ran off into the woods, only coming back after finding his way into a muddy pond. To say I was not best pleased would be putting it mildly. Later on, you may wish to try the dry shampoo method, which does work very well. After dusting the dog with dry shampoo powder, use hot, wet towels to rub it well into the coat. A spray containing dog shampoo and water can also be effectively used in this way.

PRESENTATION AND HANDLING

On the day of the show, carefully choose your clothing so that you will enhance the appearance of your dog in the ring. A scruffy handler will not do justice to a clean dog. Check that even your shoes are clean and the lead is presentable. Some people even take a change of clothing to a show which they pop into after grooming. Allow yourself plenty of time in order to find the venue, to groom and settle the dog and to get organised.

A catalogue collected at the entrance to the show will advise you of the ring and a notice board will tell you where the breed is benched. The catalogue will give your bench number. There is nothing worse than someone who arrives late, dragging an ungroomed dog into the show ring. The inevitable usually happens and the dog does a 'woopsie'.

Take a sponge and water just to rub over the coat and remove any surplus dust. Brush to tone up the coat, finely combing round the ears, hocks and featherings. A spray of fine water on its own will harden up the coat.

Allow the dog time to rest before his class. When entering the show ring, collect your number from the steward if it has not already been placed on your bench. Try and keep calm. This will help the dog not to become nervous. Avoid getting crowded out or hidden away in a corner. Always keep your eye on the judge, so you can ensure your dog is showing his best when the judge is looking your way. You should watch how the exhibitors before you are told to move their dogs by the judge, i.e. round the ring, in a triangle, straight up and down, so you know just what is expected of you.

When moving, hold the lead as loosely as possible in the left hand. This is so that the dog will move with a natural action. If the lead is too high, the dog will jump up; too short, and the dog will try and pull away at the neck, not being allowed freedom of movement. If your dog is inclined to be a timid shower he may well drop his tail. Move him around, talk to and encourage him. Place the tail over the back and gently tickle at the base. All these ploys help, given time and patience. Allow him to rest while the judge is not directly concerned with him, but carefully watch when the judge comes near.

There are some dogs who are excitable by nature and who will bark in the show ring. It is sometimes difficult to deal with this situation since it is in the dog's basic nature. As it is impossible to sanction this dog in the show ring, it should be taken back to training classes and corrected there with stern rebukes such as shaking its ruff and a clear "No". If you are pulled out by the judge into the final line-up, continue to keep your dog on his toes, since quite often a judge will change places in a line-up at the last minute.

SHOW RESULTS
Always try your hardest to win – but if you do not, there is always another day and another show. Just try to enjoy the day whatever the result. There can only be five placings in a class and often many an excellent exhibit returns home cardless. You may not agree with the judge's placings, but do congratulate the winners or you will quickly be known as unsporting.

JUDGING THE SAMOYED
All dogs are judged to the Breed Standard. Each country has its own Breed Standard. The American and Canadian Standards are very much alike. They contain more detail than the English Standard. In the USA, dogs' feet and featherings are trimmed and also their whiskers taken off. Professional handlers tend to be used more in the USA, where it is the custom for dogs to be stacked. In the UK and in most other parts of the world, it is not usual to use professional handlers, and dogs are shown more naturally, free-standing and often baited with liver to maintain attention.

THE JUDGE'S TASK
It is a privilege to receive an appointment to judge. Accepting it means being totally honest with yourself. After arriving at the show, the judge will be given a Judging Book. This is divided into three sections. One is retained in the book for the Judge, the other two are for the Secretary and the Award Board. Each class has the number of each exhibit written in black or blue. Any dog appearing in a subsequent class is entered in red.

The judge will commence judging by walking down the line of Samoyeds, visually assessing overall balance and confirmation; sometimes the dogs will run round the ring. Each dog and handler is then brought forward to be individually examined by the judge, who

Judging at Crufts 1997. The CC winners were Ch. Zamoyski Lucky Casanova At Roybridge and Vandreem Imperial Montana who went on to become a Champion.

will first ensure that the dog is standing foursquare. A visual check will then be carried out from the front and then the rear, ensuring that feet are not turning out and that hind legs are parallel. Details such as correct length of leg, tail-carriage and height are visually noticed at this stage.

Many judges will extend a hand to the dogs, to reassure them that they are not going to be hurt. It is most important that young puppies are handled gently, since a harsh experience can put them off for life.

Starting with the head, each part of the body is examined in turn. The dog is checked for a scissor bite – that is, that the upper teeth are closely overlapping the lower teeth and set square to the jaws. Teeth will then need to be examined: they should be clean and all 42 present, although this is not mentioned in the Standard.

The head should be viewed as a wedge; look for the oblique dark eyes, medium stop and overall laughing expression. Check that the ears are set well apart on the head. Feel that the ears are thick, well furred and slightly rounded at the top. Visually check for dark pigmentation.

Move on, feeling for reach of neck and that the neck is proudly arched, blending into the shoulders. Check for 45 degree angulation. This can be done by placing the index finger of the right hand on the withers and the index finger of the left hand on the prominent bone at the top of the dog's front leg. Distance between the withers should be 1 to 1.5 inches. If the withers are too far forward, this will mean that the dog will be straight in shoulder and could also be short in the neck. Front action will suffer as a result of this, with the dog being unable to extend fully.

Check for strong bone on the front legs; it should not be fine. The feet should have plenty of cushioning and be well arched. Both view and feel the chest to ensure a good deep chest coming down to the level of the elbow. Feel for spring in the ribs which should allow for plenty of heart room. There should be a level muscular back and, on a dog, underneath, a good 'tuck-up'. There should be plenty of strength in the back quarters. Feel the thigh muscle, which should be well developed. This will tell you whether a dog has been well exercised or not.

View angles of stifle, which, again, should be 45 per cent to the ground. A male should be checked to ensure that the testicles are descended. Feel the coat texture, by rubbing it through your fingers. Ensure that there is plenty of undercoat and that the coat is standing away from the body. The front legs and hocks should have abundant featherings. A male should possess adequate 'trousers' at the rear end, and a female plenty of 'skirt'.

Coats do vary considerably. A long droopy coat is undesirable. The dog should be presented clean and well-groomed. There is nothing worse than seeing a dirty Samoyed in the ring. Assess the grooming, checking particularly for 'knots" at the base of the ears. Ensure that a dog has also been fully groomed underneath and between the back legs.

You should always be able to distinguish readily the difference between male and female. Dogs should appear masculine and bitches pretty and feminine. There are some bitches who are far too big and can appear 'doggy'. Movement is most important. To assess movement properly, the dog should be moved in a straight line, returning the same way. This way you are able to assess the correct thrusting action. There should be no shuffling, no crablike actions suggesting a looseness of shoulder, and no lameness.

Viewed from the side, it is now possible to see extended front reach and powerful thrust of the rear, in one fluid movement. Any pacing or sluggish movement should be penalised.

Finally, the colour of a dog's coat should not make any difference. Cream, biscuit, brilliant white, are all equally correct. Many judges might prefer pure white, but this should not enter into it.

CHOOSING THE WINNERS

Having completed all individual assessments on each dog, decide on your ultimate placings, on those closest to the Breed Standard, and, in your own mind, the reasons for your choice. There is always a need to justify why one dog is placed in front of another. There is nothing worse than watching a judge who is indecisive and who dithers about in the ring trying to make up their mind.

Judging in the snow of the Dolomites in Italy.

It should be made plain to an exhibitor that he or she is being placed. Clearly extend your hand to each dog chosen and line them up in the centre of the ring from left to right. Five dogs (four at Open Shows) should be chosen. When you have finished with the rest of the exhibitors, thank them before allowing them to leave the ring. The Steward will then hand out the prize cards and the judge will mark the placings in the Judging Book.

THE CRITIQUE

It will only be necessary to write a critique on the first two placings, merely noting the name of the third for the purposes of the report which should appear in *Our Dogs* and *Dog World*. Exhibitors eagerly scan these papers for a report on their dog. The critique should be straightforward and honest. Some judges include faults, others do not. There are ways of making comments without being hurtful, e.g. "coat texture not as good as No. 1.", or "would have preferred darker eye." Sometimes it is possible to come across an exciting new dog or puppy and this enthusiasm can be reflected in a written critique.

When you have completed judging all the classes, and written the critiques, the Best of Breed can now be chosen. At a Championship Show, the overall winner from each sex will be awarded a Challenge Certificate and the runner-up a reserve Challenge Certificate. Between the dog CC Winner and bitch CC Winner will be the ultimate Best of Breed. At an Open Show, a Best of Breed and Reserve Best of Breed will be chosen. It is an enormous thrill when judging at a Championship Show to see your chosen Samoyed go on to win the Group or even Best in Show.

After judging, keep the Judging Book and Catalogue in a safe place, since these details may be required from you at a later date if you are required to judge elsewhere. Remember that judges do have to have broad shoulders and they are constantly criticised. There can only be one overall winner in each class. If you truly feel you have done the job to the best of your ability, then you can leave the show well satisfied.

INTERNATIONAL JUDGING

In the UK, Northern America and Australia, dogs are judged against each other in competition.

In the USA, in order to gain a Champion title, a dog needs 20 points. Three sets of points must be obtained at a 'major'. The sets of points awarded is based on the number of dogs being shown. Dependent on the number of dogs, majors are worth 3,4 or 5 points. After all single-sex judging is completed a BW (Best of Winners) is declared and points awarded accordingly. The dog and bitch BW challenge the Champions from the Specials class for Best of Breed.

In FCI countries (Fédération Cynologique International) each dog is first assessed against the Breed Standard and given a detailed critique. They are then graded Excellent, Very good, Good etc. or 1st, 2nd, 3rd dependent on each dog's closeness to the Standard. Only dogs labelled Excellent or 1st return to compete with others graded the same.

In one class it could be that there is more than one Excellent or 1st. There must therefore be final placings in a class from these 1-5 if necessary. In an Open class at Championship level, no Champions are allowed to compete, there being a special Champion class. At Championship level in FCI Countries, the Best of Breed is awarded a CAC, which corresponds to the Challenge Certificate (CC) in the UK. This counts towards the title of a Champion in a particular country.

If a dog is considered outstanding, it can be awarded CACIB. In order for a dog to become an International Champion 4 CACIBs are required from three different judges in three countries, one being his own or country of origin.

On the Continent, it is usual for a judge to have an interpreter in the ring and the critique will be written in the language of the country by the steward. In some countries, judging starts as early as 8 a.m. An Honour prize can be awarded, not always to the first prize winner but to others in the class. Any dog awarded an Honour prize can also compete for CAC.

Particularly in Scandinavia, ribbons are used in place of prize cards. These are tied to a dog's lead. Some countries have a breeders' record book which needs to be signed. In Spain, only one dog is allowed to be entered by each exhibitor in a class. Australia features 'baby puppy" classes from three to six months and exhibitors have to stand in numerical order.

Ireland features a Green Star system. Forty Green Star points are needed in order to make a dog up to an Irish Champion (Ir. Ch.). These are awarded as follows: at a major Championship Show, stars can be obtained worth 5-10 points; to become a Champion a dog must win 4 x 5 majors under four different judges or 2 x 5 in the Breed and one Group under four judges. This system is a little complex to those outside Ireland especially as the value of Green Stars varies between 1 and 10 points dependent on exhibits shown and other factors.

8 RECORD BREAKERS

This chapter is devoted to both dogs and breeders who have achieved outstanding success within a specific category or country.

UNITED KINGDOM

ENG. & IRISH CH. GOGOLEV CORBESKY 1944-1956.
Sire: Ch. Whitestar Of Kobe
Dam: Westre
Breeder: Miss Crookshank
Owner: Mrs D. L. Perry
Won 34 CCs, a record which stood for 25 years. Had 2 BOB wins at Crufts in 1951 and 1955. Was in the last four for BIS at Crufts at ten years of age. (See Chapter Nine.)

CH. GRENADIER OF CRENSA 1969-1984, known as Scot.
Sire: Ch. Fairvilla Istvan Of Airebis
Dam: Venus Of Crensa
Breeder: John James
Handler: Betty James
Won 43 CCs and 30 Best of Breeds. Was a multi group and reserve group winner who gained his title at 21 months and won his last CC at the age of eleven.

Known for his wonderful temperament. At a contest of Champions, held at Regents Park, he went round the tables and made friends with Christopher Plummer, the actor. (See Chapter Nine.)

CH. HURKUR JINGLES 1978-1986, known as Lucky.
Sire: Herondale Boris
Dam: Samont Charmaine
Breeder: Jim Dougal

Ch. Hurkur Jingles.
Photo: David Dalton.

Owners: Carole & Jim Hamilton
Became the new Breed record holder
with 46 CCs and 35 Best of Breeds,
including BOB at Crufts 1983 and
1986. Won Best in Show at West of
England Ladies Kennel Club
Championship Show, Southern Counties
Championship Show and Birmingham
City Championship Show. No. 1. Sam in
the UK in 1981, 82, 83, 84 and 1985.
(See Experts Choice.)

CH. ZAMOYSKI LUCKY STAR OF
OSTYAK known as Oakie (1981-1993).
Sire: Ch. Hurkur Jingles
Dam: Ch. Fairvilla Silver Jewel
Breeder: Carole Hamilton
Owner: Carol Fox
The current Breed Holder with 50 CCs.
Won Best in Show at West of England
Championship Show and also Leeds
Championship Show in 1987. First
Samoyed to win the Working Group at
Crufts. (See Chapter Nine.)

CH. SNOWMYTH MIVARA known
as Vara (b.1987).
Sire: Ch. Mivasam Solo

Ch. Snowmyth Mivara.

Dam: Ch. Snowmyth Melissa
Breeder: Lesley Morgan
Owners: Val & Roly Miller
In 1996 set a new Bitch Record of 24
CCs, beating the previous record of CH.
KARA QUEEN which stood since
1938. Also acquired 25 reserve CCs and
won one Working Group.

CH. VALENTINO IMPERIAL FLYER
born February 14th 1989.
Sire: Ch. Aurora Borealis Of Samovar
At Hemshire
Dam: Tsar Princess Of Lisky
Breeder: Mrs I. M. King
Owner: Mrs V. Hampton
Handler: Andrea Kirkwood
Won his first CC at Crufts in 1993 and
went on to win the Working Group.
Made up in three straight shows. This
dog was a complete unknown. His story
is a fairy tale.
    John and Betty James, of the Crensa
Kennel, wrote about him: "Just as we
were despairing of ever seeing the true
Samoyed again, out of the blue came
Ch. Imperial Flyer. He was not as big a
dog as we see today, but his lovely
wedge-shaped head with small thick
tufted ears, together with his well
spaced, correct almond eye and smiling
expression is a joy. His coat is short,
dense harsh and stands off, with the
creamy biscuit shade as in the old
Snowland Dogs which would stand up
to Arctic weather. He is perfectly
proportioned and his movement is
superb both ways and, arguably,
the Best in the Breed today." (See
Chapter Nine.)

CH. ZAMOYSKI LUCKY CASANOVA
AT ROYBRIDGE (b.1994) known
as Topper.

Ch. Zamoyski Lucky Casanova At Roybridge, pictured after winning the N.S.S. Samoyed of the Year contest in 1997.

Sire: Ch. Pykra Spring Bear At Roybridge
Dam: Ch. Zamoyski Lucky Melissa
Breeder/Owner: Bridget Enticott
Handler: Donna Fleming
Top Samoyed 1996, 1997, 1998; Top Working Dog, 1997 and Top Sire 1997 & 1998. Winner of 34 CCs and 5 Reserve CCs, 27 BOBs, 2 BIS (All Breeds), 4 BIS (Speciality), 8 Group Wins, including BOB and Group Winner Crufts 1997. Northern Samoyed Society Samoyed of the Year 1996 and 1997. South West Contest of Champions Winner 1997.

ROYBRIDGE LUCKY LEGACY
known as Smartie (b.1997).
Sire: Ch. Zamoyski Lucky Casanova At Roybridge
Dam: Astutus Advent Morn
Breeder: Bridget Enticott
Owner: Bridget Enticott/ Donna Fleming

Handler: Donna Fleming
First Samoyed to win the National Dog World/Beta Pup of the year competition in 1998.
Carole Hamilton of Zamoyski Kennels: *Our Dogs* Top Breeder Working Group 1998. (The first time a Samoyed had topped the Working Group and also the last, since at the beginning of 1999 the Samoyed was placed in the Pastoral Group.)

ROYBRIDGE STRIKE IT LUCKY
known as Jazz, born February 2nd 1997.
Sire: Ch. Zamoyski Lucky Casanova At Roybridge
Dam: Astutus Abracadabra At Roybridge
Breeder: Mrs B. Enticott
Owner: Mrs H. Mock
First Samoyed dog to obtain a Junior Warrant under the new Kennel Club regulations and take part in the JW Competition at Birmingham in 1998.

Roybridge Strike It Lucky.
Photo: Bill Welsh.

CH. SNOSCENE KALINDI OF KOBE known as Dandy.
Sire: Fairvilla White Chief
Dam: Carron Of Kobe
Breeder/Owners: Geoff & Dorothy Perkins
Was the first Samoyed to be made Best In Show at an All Breeds Championship Show, one in which there were 7,477 dogs entered. Won 18 CCs.

CH. POLAR LIGHT OF FARNINGHAM
Took the Dog CC five years in succession at Crufts in 1925, 1926, 1927, 1928, 1929.

UNITED STATES OF AMERICA

The first Samoyed to win BIS in the USA was SWEET MISSY OF SAMMAR, handled by breeder/owner Mrs Joseph J. Marshall at Toledo Kennel Club in 1949. In 1984 Jack Price and a team of five Bubbling Oaks Show Dogs were the first Samoyed team to compete the Canadian Long Distance Championship Race at Marmora.

AM. CAN. BAH. CH. POLAR MIST DOCTOR PEPPER known as Pepper, 1978-1993.
Sire: Ch. Belaya's Sergeant Pepper
Dam: Ch. Pepsi Kola Of Polar Mist
Breeder: Lynette Hanson
Co-owners: John & Kathy Ronald and Lynette Hansen Blue.
During his life he became the top owner-handled Samoyed in United States breed history. He won 13 Bests in Show, 145 Group Placements, and 8 Specialty Shows, and earned 5 National Awards of Merit at SCA Specialties. At 11 years of age he was SCA Top Stud Dog.

WORLD/INT./PUERTO RICAN AM. CAN. CH. HOOF N' PAWS A ROSE IS A ROSE whelped March 12th 1993, known as Ana Rose.
Sire: Am. Can. Ch. Hoof n' Paw's Knight Shadow, Biss & Group Winner.
Dam: Am. Can. Ch. Hoof n'Paw's Ramblin' Rose, Biss & Group Winner.
Breeder: Mardee Ward-Fanning
Owners: Jeff & Nan-Eisley Bennett and Mardee Ward-Fanning
Handler: Robert Chaffin
Ana's achievements have made her the all-time Top Winning Female in Breed history in the United States. She was No.1 Samoyed in the United States in 1996 and 1997. Two-time pedigree award winner (1996 & 1997) for most Samoyeds defeated in a year (over 2,200 dogs beaten in 1997). Ana won 9 All Breed Best in Shows and 9 specialty Best in Shows and was ranked No.6 Working Dog in 1997. Ana was exhibited three times at New York's Westminster Kennel Club. She was Best Opposite Sex in 1996 and 1998 and BOB in 1997. Ana is strongly line-bred to the famous English import CH. KISKAS KARAHOLME

World Int. Puerto Rican Am. Can. Ch. Hoof n' Paws A Rose Is A Rose.

CHEROKEE, known as PAINTER imported to America in 1972 by Breeder/Judges/ Authors Robert and Dolly Ward.

CH. MARTINGATE SNOWLAND TAZ 1944-1956.
Sire: Ivanoff Of Snowland
Dam: Eng. Ch. Bettina Marie
Owner: Dr William Ivens
Achieved four successive BOBs at the Westminster Show. Had three group firsts at Chicago, Harrisburg and Camden. Sired twenty-eight Champions including AM.CH. SWEET MISSY OF SAMMAR. Taz was twice winner of the Wimundstrev Trophy.

INT. WORLD MEX. AM. CH. NORTHWIND'S RISING STAR 1985-1998, known as Star.
Sire: Ch. Snowdahl's Budding Star
Dam: Ch. Northwind's Sugar 'n' Spice
Breeder: Jack Feinberg
Owners: Esther & Robert Halmi
Handler: Jack Feinberg
Perhaps the world's most travelled showdog. BIS winner in six countries: Israel 1987, Peru 1988, Hungary, Austria, Mexico and the USA. Back-to-back Best In Show at the World Dog Show – a record that appears unbroken.

AM. CH. QUICKSILVER'S RAZZ MA TAZZ 1981 known as Tazz.
Sire: Ch. Kolinka Quilted Bear
Dam: Ch. Quicksilver's Lucky Starr
Breeders: Danny and Chris Middleton
Owners: Danny & Chris Middleton and Eugene & Joyce Curtis
Handler: Roy Murray
The Top Winning American Samoyed in 1983 and 1984. No.1 Working Dog

in 1983 and 1984. Won 54 All Breed Best in Shows, 232 BOB, 202 Group placements. The Top Winning Samoyed of all time.

CH.WINTERFROST'S GYRFALCON known as Gyr (b.1991).
Sire: Ch. Wolf River's Eagle
Dam: Ch. Winterfrost's Moonlighting
Breeder/Owner/Handler:
Louise O'Connell
Won his first BOB at 6 months. Holds the all-time breed record for Speciality wins (BISS), numbering 12. Was ranked No.1 in the North East All Breed and Breed in 1995, 1996 and 1997. Was the Samoyed Quarterly No.1 Stud dog in 1996 and has sired over 30 Champions.

JANICE HOVELMANN of SANORKA.
In 1996 she owned both the Top Stud Dog AM.CH. SANORK'S MOONLIGHT GAMBLER (who

Ch. Winterfrost's Gyrfalcon.

was also Top Stud Dog for 1991, 1994, 1995 & 1997) and the 2nd Top Stud Dog, his son AM. CAN. CH. SANORKA'S MOONLITE TRIP'T REN J. Quite an honour.

AUSTRALIA

AUS. GRAND CH. ELGIANTO HEZA STAR.
Sire: Aust. Ch. Varson Christmas Star
Dam: Aust. Ch. Zamora Jestine Jade
Breeder/Owner: Julie Oates
No.1 Samoyed in Victoria and in dog utility group in Victoria. Only Samoyed to be a finalist in Victoria's Top Dog Show of the Year. First Samoyed to gain Grand Champion title. Stephen and Helen Gabb's Sever Kennels foundation bitch.

AUST. CH. SHEROLA LASKA ROMANOV CD CDX was the first dual-titled Samoyed bitch in Australia.

Also the first Samoyed to be placed at the Australian National Obedience Trials, in 1972. 1992 First registered litter using frozen semen; this was from a Canadian sire, CH. ORENOPAC'S CHAENA.

CANADA

AM. CAN. CH. TAKENAK'S MAKE MY DAY known as Cally.
Sire: Am. Can. Ch. Romsey's Lord Of The Rings
Dam: Am. Can. Ch. Takenak's Jani
Breeder/Owners: Drs Leslie Jocelyn & Lawrence Homik
Winner of 9 Canadian BIS and 4 BISS. Top owner-handled Samoyed in Canadian history, shown by Lawrence Homik,
and the only Samoyed to win the Samoyed Association of Canada Specialty 3 times. No.1 Samoyed in Canada 1993.

Aust. Grand Ch. Elgianto Heza Star.

Am. Can. Ch. Takenak's Make My Day.

CAN. AM. CH. BOBMARDEN'S
SPLENDID SURVIVOR CD
known as Aziza.
The first Samoyed in North America to
win a fly-ball title.

BLAIR & JUDI ELFORD:
VANDERBILT SAMOYEDS.
The Vanderbilt Kennel has thrice
been Top Samoyed Breeder in
Canada, achieving a total of 9 Best in
Show awards. They have bred/owned
46 Champions, many Group and Best
Puppy in Show winners, 1 CDX,
several CDs, Therapy, Agility and Sled
working dogs throughout North and
South America and Europe.

BIS BISS CDN AM. CH.
SNOWGHOSTS GO BETTER WITH
COKE ROMC known as Coke.
Sire: Ch. Brydawn Cyan
Snowghost Cd
Dam: Ch. Tuschany's Silver Fantasy
Rom
Breeder/Owners: Mike & Lee Anne
Palutke
The most winning Canadian Samoyed
in history, going No.1 Samoyed Puppy
in Canada in 1989, No.1 Samoyed in
Canada in 1991, No.1 Samoyed
in Canada and No.13 All Breeds in
1992 and received No.2 Stud Dog
award in the US in 1995.

CH. SNOWGHOSTS DANCE THE
TIDE known as Dancie.
Sire: Ch. Snowghosts Go Better
With Coke, Rom
Dam: Ch. Wintermist Lady Mishka
The only female in Canada to have
won Best in Show while a puppy at
ten months.

BIS BISS CDN Am. Ch. Snowghosts Go
Better With Coke.

SHEBASKA'S SULAYKHA
PAKOVA CD.
Breeder/Owners: Frank & Helga Gruber
Following winning The Samoyed Club
of America's top obedience Samoyed
award in the 1970s, went on to earn
The Dog World award for canine
distinction with 3 consecutive scores
of 195.5, 197.5 and 198 and won four
successive HIT (High in Trials) awards
at All Breed Shows.

CAN. AM. CH. ORENPAC'S
CHAENA.
Top Dog in Canada for 3 years, sire
of 26 Champions.

DENMARK

DISCO'S BEAUTIFUL GIRL.
Junior World Winner in Bruxelles 1995.
BOB and World Winner, Helsinki.
World Winner, Vienna 1996. Top
Samoyed Bitch 1995, 1996, 1997
and 1998.
Best in Show winner in Denmark
and Germany.

Dan. Sw. Nord. Ch. Cabaka's Gino Of Apollon.

DAN. SW. NORD. CH. CABAKA'S GINO OF APOLLON
Sire: Kaissas Leto Apollon
Dam: Cabaka's Anais Of Ice Prince
Breeder: Gitta Morrell
Owner: Birgit Danielson
BIS at the Bundessieger, Germany's largest show, in 1998. Also Best Male Samoyed in Denmark in 1998.

NEW ZEALAND

The first New Zealand Champion was:
NZ CH. DOCTOR born May 1915
Sire: Coona
Dam: Nova
Breeder: Mr R. Thornton
Owner: Mrs Richards
Of Wellington
He was registered as an Esquimaux and exhibited as a Samoyed.

The first dual-titled AUST. & NZ CHAMPIONS were:
KALIA KUTS and KALINA

STARDUST born 30.11.57
Breeder: Mrs Y. Sydenham-Clarke.

AUS. & NZ CH. KALINA SMIRNOFF
Sire: Eng. Aus. NZ Ch. Darryl Of Tamitsa
Dam: Ch. Starya Of Kobe
Breeder: Y. Sydenham-Clarke
Owner: Neilma Fraser
At the New Zealand Speciality Show was Best in Show on 4 occasions.

SWEDEN

CH. NORDVIKENS AWASHKA and her son CH. NORDVIKENS TSAR DODOOROWITCH.
First dogs to gain the title Svensk Polarhundchampion – a Working Championship introduced in 1993.

Such, Nuch, Intuch S (Polar) Ch. Ntch Nordvikens Awashka.

9 EXPERTS' CHOICE

I asked several judges to name their all-time favourite Samoyed. Their choices are fascinating and cover the international scene. They are also a testimony to the judges' ability to know quality when they see it. I am starting this chapter with my own favourite, who was Ch. Hurkur Jingles, known as Lucky.

In 1995, I wrote the following about this dog for *Dog World*: "Lucky was a once-in-a-lifetime dog and I fear we shall never see his like again. He was bought as a pet by Jim and Carole Hamilton from Jim Dougall, who bred this dog in a first litter which also contained two Champions. This Samoyed was quite outstanding and completely dominated the Samoyed world in his heyday in the 1980s. He won everything in sight and accrued 46 CCs before his untimely death at eight years. A true showman, he possessed superb style. He excelled in head quality, exhibiting the true Samoyed smile. He had a marvellous coat – and, in fact, had it all. He may have been a shade too tall for some, but he was a dog who passed many of his qualities on to his progeny. There will never be a perfect dog, but this one came pretty close."

ROBERT H. WARD (USA)
"I have thought long and hard over this. I have been judging for 45 years so I have seen a wide spectrum of dogs. Twenty-five years ago in England, there was a bitch called Ch. Fairvilla Katrina. She possessed the correct proportions, type, style and good movement and the correct attitude towards life and people. For an outstanding one in the USA, I would have to select Ch. Staryvna Of Snowland, who was, for me, a duplicate of Ch. Fairvilla Katrina. This bitch was the first to win a National Specialty in the USA. I feel that she was as close to the original dogs as possible. Her pedigree in one line had only four generations. Ch. Kara Sea, her grandfather, was twelve when he sired her father, who was also twelve, thus going back 24 years. She had only one litter but six of her eight puppies became Champions.

"A great male in England, I shall always remember, was Ch. Grenadier Of Crensa. He had a great head and body with

92

Ch. Grenadier Of Cresna.
Photo: F. E Garwood, reproduced by kind permission of Dog World.

typical Samoyed smile and personality. Of the males in the USA, there was Ch. Quick Silvers Razz Ma Tazz, with an impossible show record of fifty-four Best in Shows and two National Specialties. He was neither the largest or the smallest in the show ring. His size and proportions were superb and his movement was spectacular, and this attitude was faultless. He was as steady as a rock and a good ambassador for the breed.

"The other male who was very impressive in the USA was Ch. Kiskas Karaholme Cherokee, who we imported from England. He finished quite rapidly and became a tremendous stud force. In a single litter with Ch. Iceways Ice Cube he produced three males and two bitches. Two of the males became Champions and both won All Breed Best in Shows. The unbelievable fact is that one of the males sired one hundred and forty-two Champions and the other sired fifty-five before he was killed. These two dogs put a tremendous pressure upon the breed in the USA, for they created the long upper arm which the Samoyed breed needed all over the world. At the present time, while I have not judged her in the ring,

Ana – Ch. Hoof N' Paws A Rose Is A Rose – has it all in one package: size 21", breed type, gait and correct attitude towards life and people. She has won more All Breed Shows than any other Samoyed bitch, including 11 Samoyed Breed Specialties and a National Breed Specialty with an entry of 590 with 120 Champions.

JEAN LANNING – UK all rounder judge.
She chose Aust. Ch. Samdreena Sarah's Girl, owned by Mr and Mrs Wooley and handled by daughter Jenny McCullough. She was awarded BIS at the Brisbane Royal Show in 1997. Jean says "She was quite lovely and went back to British breeding. My best dog was her brother – Aust. Ch. Samdreena Maori Chief."

IVOR MUNDAY – SAMOVAR
Ivor has almost half a century of experience within the breed. He has judged in New Zealand and Australia and bred/owned 10 Champions.
"My all-time best Samoyed was Mrs D. L. Perry's Ch. Gogolov Corbesky. Although not bred in Mrs Perry's famous Kobe Kennels, he was campaigned by her after she bought him. He was being shown in the early 1950s and gained 34 CCs. He was the nearest to the Standard that I have ever seen and one of my ambitions was to breed Sams as close to him as possible. He was also a dog that was capable of a day's work on the Tundra."

JOAN LUNA (USA)
Joan has had Samoyeds since the early 1970s. As well as judging other breeds, she now judges Samoyeds internationally.

"I would like to nominate Ch. Sitkins Simply Scrumptious (BIS, BISS), known as 'Scarlet' , as my choice. She was by Ch. Blue Sky's Simply Smashing out of Ch. Sitkins Stardust Melody, and bred by Dick and Christine Higley. Her dates are April 16th 1985 to November 6th 1999. In her career she won 150 BOBs, 70 Group placements, and seven BIS. At her last show, as a veteran, she defeated over 2000 dogs. She was top winning bitch at the Samoyed Club of America in 1989. She won awards of Merit in 1987, 1988 and 1991. Included in her pedigree is Ch. Kolinka's Quilted Bear, who was the sire of Ch. Quicksilver's Razz Ma Tazz, top winning Samoyed in American history. Her pedigree also traces back to the English import Ch. Kiskas Karaholme Cherokee. Scarlet was mated only once, to Ch. Image's The Barrister, and produced six Champions."

BETTY McHUGH (CANADA)

Betty is an international Judge who has been involved with Samoyeds since 1950. She has judged the breed in Canada, the USA and Australia. Also since 1974, she has been an All Breed Obedience Judge, training Samoyeds to achieve their Obedience titles and also working Samoyeds in harness. She says:

" I believe Am. Can Iceway's Ice Breaker, bred by Mike and Bobby Smith of Arkansas, sired by English import Ch. Kiskas Karaholme Cherokee out of Ch. Iceways Ice Cube, to be one of the greatest dogs produced on this continent and one of the best producers. He was superbly built, which made him a good mover and was surpassed in both areas only by his dam. Used extensively in the 70s and 80s, he produced well, however, few had the knowledge to hold the quality in their breeding programs.

"This period produced many excellent Samoyeds in North America among whom Ch. K-Ways Omen Of Destiny CD, bred by Bob and Wanda Krauss, stands out. I feel also that Silveracres Sir Glokon, bred by Harold and Doris McLaughlin and owned in Canada by Islay Aitchinson, to be the most structurally sound Samoyed I have ever seen.

"I have awarded BIS to only two Samoyeds, who were both good bitches. First was Am. & Can. Ch. Jasam's Rocky Mountain High, bred and owned by Sarah and Jack Post, and Can. Ch. Vanderbilt's Break the Seal, bred and owned by Blair and Judi Elford. Another bitch I really admire is Ch. Aldonza Kiss And Tell CD, bred by Fay Tucker, who I gave Best of Breed out of a large entry in Melbourne, Australia."

MARGARET WILCOCK – ANNECY

Margaret has a wealth of experience and has judged the breed in many parts of the world. "My nomination would be Eng. Ir. Ch. Gogolov Corbesky. He was a great dog of his time. When he entered the ring with his owner, Mrs D.L.Perry, both were immaculately presented. He was a dog who had very great presence."

ROBIN LINGS – DELMONTE

Robin is a Breed specialist who has travelled widely, once working in Italy for an Italian Count. "For my nomination of Best Samoyed dog, specifically based on achievement, without reserve or embarrasment, I would name World Int. Ch. Delmonte This Is It. Following his BOB at Crufts in 1972, he was exported to the USA, where he notched up 75 Group wins and sired over 100 Champions. In the UK

Muriel Hopkin receiving her award for outstanding service to the Samoyed breed.

my choice of best Samoyed dog ever would be Ch. Grenadier Of Crensa, bred and owned by John and Betty James. In his era, he held the record for most CCs won. He was a magnificent specimen all round and excelled in movement. I would nominate Mrs Danvers's Ch. Fairvilla Anastasia as the best bitch. A most profound and exquisite biscuit-shaded Sammie. She held her own, all the way through until her late teens when she was still winning, just like a youngster."

MURIEL HOPKIN – CROWNIE
Muriel is the winner of the 1998 Northern Samoyed Society's Gold Medal Award for outstanding service to the Samoyed breed. "I would nominate Ch. Hurkur Jingles as the best dog. I know

he was a big dog – but all of a piece. A splendid sire and it takes a big dog to start a good line. He was bred by Mr J. Dougall and had a lovely temperament."

ROSE LEWIS – SNOWCRYST
Rose is a highly respected doyen of the Samoyed breed.
  "I consider Ch. Snowcryst Sakel as one of the best dogs. He had a lovely temperament and his coat was so thick, there was enough undercoat to make another coat with. He had lovely featherings and feet and overall was superb. His sister, Ch. Snowcryst Anibras, is to me the nearest to the Standard. Both these two were pale biscuit with pure white tails and pants. All my stock came down from these, including some of the best white ones with the lovely silver tips."

JOHN AND BETTY JAMES –
CRENSA. Breed Specialists.

John, in particular, now judges many other breeds, both in the UK and around the world. Betty is widely known for her judging and handling abilities.

John writes: "Twenty-five years or so ago I was asked to write on the best Samoyed I had ever seen – and now, after over forty years and hundreds of dogs seen I have been asked the same question. Every decade a really great dog seems to appear almost out of the blue and each one of them has the very special attributes one longs to see, and to be part of that time when he or she is at their best. I will not fall into the trap of saying dogs today are not as good as they used to be or that the dogs of today are better than those of yesteryear. There have been some great dogs over this lifespan.

"There are two outstanding bitches that have left an enduring impression. The first was when I had been showing for about a year in 1960. Her name was Ch. Snowland Verna, she was about five years old. I thought she was the most beautiful bitch one would ever wish to see; she had such a lovely gentle kind expression that made you just want to touch her and give her a hug and never let go. Even today after all these years I can still picture her with the lovely magnificent white coat with the silver tips shimmering in the sunlight with not a hair out of place. She was owned by Mrs Goldsmith who lived in Jersey. In all she won 12 CCs, a very fine achievement, and there were far fewer sets of CCs on offer in those days. I was just embarking upon a show and breeding career, and such was the lasting impression this bitch had on me that I

Ch. Valentine Imperial Flyer, pictured with handler Angela Kirkwood and judge Pamela Cross-Stern.

decided to include Snowland lines into the Crensa pedigrees.

"Almost twenty years later, Betty and I both agree that probably the best bitch we have ever had the pleasure of going over and awarding the CC was Ch. Northcape Simona Of Annecy. We feel she was the very ideal in type, size, excellent overall conformation with the correct type coat; and, always superbly handled and presented – the lovely feminine head with the happy Sammy smile was captivating.

"In males, Betty had no hesitation in nominating Ch. Whitewisp Lunar Module, bred and owned by Mrs B. Grounds: a superbly balanced dog with a classic masculine head, he was of the correct size and his harsh stand-off coat was eye-catching. As a stud dog, he became invaluable to the breed, the sire of ten Champions, certainly an icon of his time during the 1970s.

"After giving a lot of thought to what I considered the best male I have ever seen or judged, I turn to the judging of Crufts 1993. A dog came into the Limit class and neither the dog or handler had I ever seen before – nor had the majority of spectators at the ringside. As he came in, it was as though the clock had been turned back thirty years – my "dream" dog, a "Snowland" dog. I thought, if he moves as well as he looks, the class is his for the taking. Some might have described him as on the small side against the majority of today's dogs; he was not – he was the correct, ideal size. The head and expression was incredible, pure "Snowland", the coat, short, harsh textured, stand-off with colour just slightly shaded, not the soft pure white we are so used to seeing today. Then the movement; because he was so perfectly built all through, the perfect size, movement from the rear, in profile and the front was the best I can ever remember. He went on to win the Crufts Working Group, had a dramatic 1993, made up in three straight Shows and further Group wins. His name was Ch. Valentine Imperial Flyer. It was a great climax to my Samoyed career to have 'found' him."

FERELITH SOMERFIELD (UK)
International all-rounder judge and Chairman of Dog World Ltd.
"It is always difficult to choose one example of a breed as one's all-time favourite, but even more so if one is a non-breed-specialist judge, as opposed to someone who is closely involved with the breed and sees the top dogs and bitches constantly. When a non-breed-specialist is lucky enough to get a chance to judge, it could be that the best of breed chosen is not in full coat on that day. Although coat is an important factor in judging the breed, Samoyeds can drop coat at any time. Indeed, some males can actually lose weight when a bitch in the household is in season. Conversely, at that same show a certain dog, or bitch, can look the best they have ever done and they never attain quite the same excellence again.

"Breed specialists see the dogs on many occasions and so are in a far better position to make a balanced judgement. They also know exactly what the dogs have achieved at stud or in the nursery. Someone like me can find out the statistics, but I cannot know whether, for

Ch. Zamoyski Lucky Star Of Ostyak, pictured here after winning his first CC.

example, a dog has consistently produced quality stock only to the best bitches, or whether they can do the same when used to mediocre bitches.

"Through the years a number of Samoyeds have thrilled me, and not all of them have come from the UK. I shall always remember Ch. Northwind's Rising Star who I made Best Of Breed at Chicago in 1987. I thought he was a superb dog and I know he had considerable success in Group and Best In Show competition. He was owned by Ester Halmi, bred by Jack Feinberg and Helen Feinberg, handled by Jacob Feinberg, and was by Ch. Snowdahl's Budding Star ex Ch. Northwind Sugar and Spice.

"I have also seen some lovely Samoyeds in Australasia, the latest being a quality young bitch called NZ Ch. Kimchatka Laced With Ice, imported from Australia, bred by E. Maitland and Mr and Mrs D. Brown and owned by G. A. Grey and J. Hawkins. She was by Aust. Ch. Kimchatka Touch Of Class ex Aust. Ch. Mihalichenka La Contessa and I was delighted to make her Best In Show at the New Zealand Kennel Club's National show in September 1998.

"However, for my favourite of all time I am coming back to the UK and Ch. Zamoyski Lucky Star Of Ostyak. I first saw him at the Welsh Kennel Club show in 1983 where, although he was still very young, I gave him his first CC. The next time I judged him was in the Working Group at Crufts in 1988. For me he stood away, showing and moving to perfection, his coat gleamed and he had everything I wanted in a top-class Samoyed. After I had given him the Group, his owner, Mrs Fox, told me I had already given him a CC. I thought it

was the first time I had seen him! He was, in fact, best of breed twice at Crufts and won numerous CCs over several years under both specialist and non-specialist judges. He was a credit to his breeder, Mrs Hamilton, and to his sire, the big-winning Ch. Hurkur Jingles, and his dam Ch. Fairvilla Silver Jewel, as well as his owner who campaigned him fearlessly."

GERALD MITCHELL – KISKAS
UK International breed specialist and all-rounder.
"Having time to reflect on what would be my expert's choice, many good Samoyeds come to mind. Many great dogs like Ch. Hukur Jingles, Ch. Fairvilla Fairfax, Ch. Kalman Airebis and Ch. Grenadier of Crensa must linger in one's memory as Samoyeds to reflect on and debate. But to my mind two great British champions have to be Ch. Snowking Of Carwood as a male, and Ch. Crownie Cor Corelli Of Equinox as a bitch.

"Ch. Snowking Of Carwood, born in 1955, was a fine masculine dog and had great presence. He held the title of breed record holder, winning 24 CCs, 24 Reserve CCs and 18 Best of Breeds. His progeny included many well-known British Champions. To name a few: Ch. Fairvilla Istvan of Airebis, Ch. Kalman of Airebis, Ch. Grenadier Of Crensa and American Champion Kiskas Karaholme Cherokee, plus many others which had direct links with his lines. He was a great Samoyed and one that should be remembered. He was a great credit to his breeder and owner, Gladys Varney.

"Ch. Crownie Cor Corelli Of Equinox, born in 1961, would have to be my choice as the most feminine of all

*Ch. Crownie Cor
Corelli Of Equinox.*

bitches. I watched her on many occasions. She stood out. She was pretty and very typy. She had all the characteristics that one would want in a Samoyed bitch. She won eight CCs in all, always making her presence felt. She possessed a beautiful coat, gleaming white, and her dark eyes and pigment complemented her great attractiveness. Maggie, as she was known, was never bred from, which was a great pity, but the memory of her should not be forgotten as her breeding came from a consistent line of beautiful bitches, something for which the Hopkin family and their Crownie kennel became very famous.

These two Samoyeds were sired by Kim of Crownie, making them half-brother and sister. Without doubt these breeding lines have had a tremendous effect on the present-day Samoyed as we know it. They have influenced many great dogs and bitches in the UK, America and many other countries worldwide. I am privileged to have personally known them both."

JOHN RONALD (USA)

John is twice a past President and Treasurer of the Samoyed Club of America of which he has been a member for 25 years. For 12 years he has been the American Kennel Club Delegate. He has been an American Kennel Club Licenced Judge for 13 years. His choice is Ch. Polar Mist Cover Gyrl Of Lazys, known as Shelby.

He says: "On several occasions, I have judged our National Specialty. On the second occasion, I was quite excited when I found a young bitch that typified the proper qualities of size, structure, movement and type. Shelby is a natural showdog, enjoying the show experience from beginning to last, always free and natural. Her movement and attitude were exemplary and impressed me from the moment she entered my ring. When I awarded her the Winner's ribbon, it completed her American Championship. She has since gone on to win six Specialty competitions and has won several all-breed show Groupcompetitions as well as a number of other group placements."

Ch. Skardu's Kass White Star.

Kass White Star who won Expo Mundial in 1991 in Dortmund and Valencia in 1992 respectively."

NEILMA FRASER (NEW ZEALAND)
Neilma is both a breed specialist and an all-breeds judge.
"I thought long and hard about this. Initially I nominated Eng. Aust. NZ Ch. Darryl Of Tamitsa since he was much valued for the enormous influence he had on the breed both in New Zealand and Australia. However, I felt that his son, Aus. NZ Ch. Kalina Smirnoff was even better and also did a great deal for the breed in New Zealand. He had a longer length of leg than his father and was a fine upstanding and glamorous dog who moved beautifully."

RENATA FOSSATI (ITALY)
She did not feel able to single out one particular dog but stressed that among the qualities a dog must have, such as a typical head, right proportions and correct coat, there must be right movement. This was a feature which must not be forgotten or compromised, so that we remain true to the Breed Standard and the early founders, Mr and Mrs Kilburn-Scott.

ANTONIO V. CHOYA (SPAIN)
"El. Ch. Skardu's Iberian Bear was a great dog bred by myself, winning many prizes, but he no longer belongs to me! Ch. Clan's Banko, acquired in Italy, who was a great Champion, siring twenty Champions – and two of his daughters, Ch. Skardu's Katerina and Ch. Skardu's

Neilma Fraser awarded BIS to Aust. Ch. Aldonza Kistas Kid at the New South Wales Ch. Show 1994.

10 *HEALTH CARE*

At some time in their lives, all dogs will suffer from a problem or illness, and the Samoyed is no exception. I have endeavoured to list those that spring to mind for information purposes but inclusion does not mean the problem is endemic to the breed.

ACID MILK
Such milk produced by a poorly bitch can be dangerous for young puppies. It is possible that they could die from starvation and constipation. The puppies will feel cold and look full. They will lie away from their mother and cry, which will distress her.

Action: It is possible to test for this condition using litmus paper. The milk of a healthy bitch is neutral or very slightly acid: using blue litmus paper there will be no change in colour. With acid milk the litmus paper will change to bright pink. Keep the puppies warm and contact the vet. The puppies can be given warm water with a few drops of milk of magnesia. They should be given a replacement milk feed until their mother is fully recovered.

ANAL GLAND INFECTION
Sometimes this infection can occur when the anal glands, which produce a smelly fluid and which lie in sacs either side of the anus, become blocked.

Signs and symptoms: The dog may attempt to bite or chase his tail or "scoot" by rubbing his bottom against the ground.

Action: The glands may need to be emptied from time to time at the vet's without using anaesthetic. Feed more bulk to the diet. Seek veterinary advice sooner rather than later.

ARTHRITIS
Inflammation of the joints causing stiffness. A breed survey suggests this can occur later in life.

Signs and symptoms: A dog might have some difficulty getting to its feet, but seems easier when moving. There could be some weight loss.

Treatment: Homeopathy and acupuncture can be moderately successful. Surgery may be required.

Action: Consult with your vet.

Bred for a working life in harsh conditions, the Samoyed tends to be a hardy breed that suffers few serious health problems.

AUTOIMMUNE DISORDER

This is the name used for any disease in which the immune system, which normally fights any invading bacteria and viruses, turns against the body itself. Bitches tend to be more often affected than dogs. The cause is thought to be the result of a faulty gene. Luckily the condition is rare in the Samoyed breed.

Signs and symptoms: These vary. It is a complicated condition causing such effects as rheumatoid arthritis in the joints, eye or severe skin problems.

BLOCKED TEAR DUCT

Tears, which lubricate the eyes, are drained by the lacrymal duct. If this duct is too narrow or blocked the tears cannot be drained properly and they may run down the side of the face, causing staining or inflammation of the skin. Sometimes seen in young puppies.

Action: Seek advice from your vet.

CANCER

One of the biggest causes of death in dogs generally. Many dogs over the age of ten develop cancer. Commonest problems are mammary tumours in bitches and tumours of the skin.

CRYPTORCHIDISM

One or both testicles fail to descend. Thought to affect about 4 per cent of puppy dogs.

DIABETES

Unfortunately found quite frequently in the Samoyed breed in the UK. There are two forms: Diabetes Mellitus and Diabetes Insipidus.

Diabetes Mellitus occurs when sugars are not properly broken down in the pancreas by the hormone, insulin, which controls the amount of sugar in the blood. This causes blood sugar to be excreted in the urine.

Diabetes Insipidus occurs due to deficiency of the anti-diuretic hormone, which is necessary for the kidneys to function normally in reabsorbing water.

Signs and symptoms: Seems to occur more in bitches than dogs, usually around seven years of age or later. Very occasionally it can be diagnosed at a younger age of around three years. Bitches may need to be spayed because of hormonal imbalance. There will be increased urination and excessive thirst. There may be some weight loss, and eyesight can be affected.

Action: Seek veterinary advice early if symptoms are seen. Left too late the condition can become chronic. Diabetic Samoyeds can live for many years with daily insulin injections. The amount of sugar in the urine can be monitored by use of a strip. Exercise should be maintained.

DIARRHOEA

It is common enough for a young puppy to suffer with this, because of changes in food and surroundings. However, there can be other causes. These could include a vitamin deficiency, enteritis caused by a virus or eating a foreign body, being unable to digest lactose-type milk, or a puppy being given adult food.

Action: Starve for 24 hours other than allowing water and glucose. Then feed white meat such as chicken and fish, also rice pudding.

DISTICHIASIS

A double row of eyelashes or extra eyelashes, some of which are turned against the eyeball. Can cause watery eyes, which in the Samoyed breed can

lead to staining. Can also lead to severe, chronic conjunctival injury.
Action: A dab of Vaseline under the eyes will help prevent this. The vet can pluck or cauterize these lashes. However, if lashes are cauterized this can damage eye-rim pigmentation, making it pink.

DISTEMPER
A disease caused by a virus invading the cells and reproducing. Since the virus enters the cells before the illness is known, it is impossible to kill off the virus without also killing off the cells. Antibiotics therefore are of no use except for secondary infection. A dog recovering from this will be immune for the remainder of its life. Puppies do receive immunity from their mothers from the first milk from her mammary glands, known as colostrum. This immunity should last until a puppy is twelve weeks of age.

ECTROPION
The eyelid turns outward and down.
Action: This condition may be difficult for the lay person to spot, but contact your vet when there appears to be any eye discomfort.

ENDOMETRITIS
Inflammation of the lining of the uterus due to infection or bacteria. Bitches can sometimes become ill after an abortion and can discharge from the vagina. Infertility in a bitch could be caused by a uterine infection.
Action: It may be necessary to remove the uterus but most cases can be treated with antibiotics.

ENTROPION (Inverted eyelids)
This is a turning in of the eye rim, a condition which occurs in the Samoyed and this can cause great discomfort. The lashes rub on the eye and this can lead to blindness. It can appear in both young puppies and older dogs and is an inherited condition.
Action: Although it can be corrected by surgery, it is advisable not to breed with such dogs since the condition can jump several generations.

EPILEPSY
This is a disorder of the central nervous system. It can be inherited, but this is by no means certain. Causes are not fully understood but the commonest cause seems to be the distemper virus. Signs that a fit is about to happen are that the dog may act strangely and may drool unnaturally before becoming very quiet. The dog might even present with facial tics. A flickering light on TV might cause a fit. The dog will collapse, shake, paddle and be unable to stand. There will be a loss of bowel and bladder control. Usually after a few minutes, the dog will return to normal. Sometimes puppies heavily infected with worms can have a form of epilepsy which is called "running fits".
Action: Shade the room and lie the dog on its side. Do not bother about the mouth since you could easily get bitten and dogs rarely choke on their tongue. Contact your vet for advice. Sometimes drugs can be used. Do not use this dog for breeding purposes.

EXTERNAL PARASITES
ECTOPARASITES (parasites that live on or in the skin).
In the main these are fleas, lice, ticks and mange mites.
Fleas are little brown wingless insects

which are usually to be found around the neck and abdomen. Sometimes they are not easily detected. Their presence is indicated when a dog is seen scratching and nipping a body part with his teeth. Treatment of both the dog and the environment is required. Seek veterinary advice should the problem persist after using flea-control remedies such as sprays, collars and pills.

Lice are fat, brown, wingless insects, which lay eggs (nits) which stick in the hair, usually being found around the neck and ears and causing frequent scratching. Washing with insecticide is required.

Ticks are rounded insects which will grow with gorging and are easily passed on by sheep or hedgehogs. The tick will bury its head into the host animal's skin. Soaking the tick in surgical spirit can loosen its hold on the skin. If the head is not removed, secondary infection can occur.

Mange mites are invisible to the naked eye and, again, cause scratching, since the mite burrows into the skin. Most commonly affected areas are underneath the thighs and forelegs and the edges of the ears. The dog's bedding needs to be destroyed and the dog treated 3 to 4 times a week.

EYE ULCERS
These can sometimes be caused by the dog running into shrubs and scratching the eye.
Signs and symptoms: Dog desperately rubbing eye with paw.
Treatment: The vet will place a green dye into the eye to establish the problem. The condition can be treated by ointment supplied by the vet. However, some cases will require an operation to scrape the surface of the eye. This will require the dog to wear a huge collar afterwards for a few days to prevent scratching, but the operation is usually successful.

FAECES EATING
A horrible habit but not a sign that anything is wrong or that the dog is diet- deficient. It probably stems from the behaviour of dogs in the wild when they would follow other animals to eat their faeces to receive some nourishment.
Action: It is up to you to discipline your dog not to eat either these faeces or cow dung.

FITS
There are at least 14 causes and many people and some vets tend to call any fit epileptic, which would not be correct.

GASTRIC TORSION AND BLOAT
A most painful and distressing condition, which can come on quite suddenly and is known to occur in large-chested breeds. It can, unfortunately, often be fatal. If this condition is suspected, it must be treated by a vet immediately and literally every minute counts. The stomach enlarges, mostly when it is full of food, and there is a build-up of gas. The stomach swings and becomes twisted (torsion) so gas cannot escape, and it becomes hard. The dog may well have difficulty in breathing.

Causes of this condition are not fully understood although research is taking place. There are many suspected causes.
1. It can occur when a large meal is bolted or eaten rapidly or if food is not pre-soaked prior to feeding, since the food can absorb liquid in the stomach and consequently swell. (Suggestions: feed two smaller meals at different parts of the day or place large stones in feeding dish to prevent rapid feeding.)
2. It could be that certain meat might be

infected by gas-forming organisms.

3. It could be brought on by exercise after feeding. (Suggestion: exercise before feeding or allow one hour to elapse after feeding before exercise.)

4. Could be brought on by drinking large amounts of water after eating dry food. (Suggestion: monitor closely).

5. Can occur where a dog does not eat on the day prior to a show and snatches at bait in the show ring, gulping down air at the same time. (Suggestion: never throw bait or liver to a dog in the show ring.)

6. Bitches after whelping and during lactation can sometimes pose a risk. (Suggestion: be alert for this.)

7. Other suspected causes are blood disorders and stress. Although cereal-based diets were looked at closely in America, gastric torsion has been found to occur with dogs fed on every type of diet.

Signs and Symptoms: The dog will wander about looking harassed and uncomfortable. The most certain way of knowing is if the dog drinks a large amount of water and is sick. The resulting vomit will look like white foam. *Note:* Unfortunately in both the UK and the USA, Samoyeds have died from this condition.

Treatment for bloat: Excess gas must be released from the stomach as soon as possible. Get to your vet straightaway. In gastric dilation, gas can be released by passing a tube down the oesophagus into the stomach. The stomach can then be washed out through this tube. In gastric torsion, where the stomach twists, it is impossible to pass a tube into the stomach to release the gas, so a hypodermic needle has to be inserted through the skin into the stomach by the vet. This will relieve the pressure in the abdomen, allowing the dog to breath more easily. In order to return the stomach to normal an operation is necessary, and the dog will have to be placed on a drip and receive intensive care. (Suggestion: to assess whether a dog is swelling more than normal after a meal, measure round the widest part of the abdomen and keep a record.)

HERNIA
Protrusion of an organ or part of an organ through an abnormal cavity. In young puppies an umbilical hernia appears. This is a swelling in the navel, soft to the touch. It will slip back when pressure is applied and, as the puppy grows, the hole will close. It is usually an inherited condition. A large hernia, or swelling in the groin should be operated on and repaired. A different hernia can be present in older dogs as a soft swelling on the side of the anus.

HIP DYSPLASIA (HD)
This is a complicated condition which occurs because of a faulty joint in one, or sometimes both, hips. It is known that the cause is genetic but environmental influences also can play a part. It is not easy to detect in young puppies. Normally, a hip joint has a deep cup-and-ball socket. With Hip Dysplasia the socket is shallow, causing a poor fit. Since the condition is not easily seen it might be some years before HD is suspected. It might only be slight, but some cases are so bad that the dog will experience great pain and become lame. In some severe cases osteo-arthritis can develop later on in life. The Kennel Club run a joint X-ray scheme with the British Veterinary Association. After 12 months

of age a dog can be tested for HD. Specialist panels examine the radiographs and report hip scores to the Kennel Club. In America, dogs are X-rayed at 24 months. Stud dog owners request that a bitch is HD-tested before mating. During the period 1983-1998, 919 Samoyeds were X-rayed, with the average score being 12.75. This is acceptable but should not cause complacency.

Note: There is sometimes a diversity of opinion on HD. Some research has indicated that when conscientious breeders were using only HD-free stock, the incidence of HD did not drop, only the severity. The quality of the breed needs to be considered along with the quality of the hips, and the best thing breeders can do is to X-ray so that as much as possible is known about each individual dog. A health screening section is now included in The Kennel Club Breeder Registration Certificate.

HYDROPS OR HYDROPS ALLANTOIS

This is a condition known to occur in Jersey cows and it does occur with some breeding bitches, although cases are rare. It is known to have occurred within the Samoyed breed in the UK, the USA, Australia and Italy. The cause is difficult to assess: it could be genetic, due to cardiac problems or arguably due to vaccinations. There is an excessive production of fluid surrounding puppies in the womb. Puppies can easily drown and quick surgical action is required.

Signs and Symptoms: Towards the end of a pregnancy, the bitch swells up and becomes abnormally large. It becomes difficult for her to lie down and breathe. The stomach becomes tight, filling with fluid, and at the full time of

pregnancy, the bitch is unable to have uterine contractions. Pressure of the fluid can cause blood vessels to burst, the womb becomes weakened and stretched by the fluid, and trying to sew this together, could be described as trying to sew cheese.

Treatment: The bitch should not be laid on her back. Most cases require a Caesarean to be undertaken.

METRITIS

Inflammation of the wall of the uterus due to bacteria or infection. Can take the form of a chronic disease. It is troublesome because there are no obvious symptoms until the bitch is bred, except possibly a slight vaginal discharge. First signs are when a bitch aborts or produces stillborn or weak pups. Examination of vaginal smears by microscope might be necessary for a diagnosis to be positive. Antibiotics usually are effective. If a bitch who has had metritis successfully produces a litter, she and the pups should receive antibiotics a few days after whelping.

OBSESSIVE-COMPULSIVE BEHAVIOUR

Most common is excessive licking and biting of feet, paws or tail. It is not really clear what causes this behaviour. It could be due to an irritation or, in some cases, to a psychological problem such as boredom, anxiety or separation. Research in America proved that antidepressants were effective in treating similar human disorders and they may well have a similar success with dogs.

PERIODONTAL OR GUM DISEASE

This is one of the most common of dental problems in dogs. It can lead to bad breath, bleeding gums and loose teeth. In progressive cases, periodontal disease can destroy bone and cause tooth loss. Watch for a build-up of plaque and accumulations of food in the teeth which foster bacteria.

Action: Brush teeth regularly but briefly. With a circular motion, brush at the gumline. Use special dog toothpaste, since human toothpaste can cause a stomach upset. Raw-hide chews provide a good cleaning action.

'THE PINK PROBLEM'

This occurs when companion dogs lick each other or when bitches lick puppies excessively. The favourite licking place is the ears and the acid contained in the saliva of the licker causes a pinkish-brownish patch to appear.

The solution: Feed a pinch of bicarbonate of soda to the dog doing the licking.

PROGRESSIVE RETINAL ATROPHY (PRA)

This is a hereditary retinal degeneration affecting the eye.

Signs and symptoms: Walking into objects, night blindness. Can lead to total blindness.

Treatment: None really successful. Usually transferred from parents who have a recessive gene. Identify affected and carrier dogs and breed only to clear dogs.

PYOMETRA

This is a life-threatening infection and can be present for months without showing symptoms. There are two types, open and closed. In both forms the uterus fills with large amounts of bacteria-infected fluids. The cause of this is not always known, but it does tend mostly to be found in older bitches. However, there are always exceptions to the rule and it can occasionally be found in a very young bitch after her first season.

Signs to watch for: Usually occurs up to six weeks after a bitch has been in season. Any male dog will become confused with the smell coming from such a bitch. The bitch becomes listless, has a vaginal discharge, drinks plenty of water and urinates frequently. In open cases, the cervix will discharge a smelly, brown pus. In cases where the cervix is closed, the bitch can become very ill.

Treatment: Veterinary treatment should be sought immediately and the bitch may have to be spayed. Only very rarely can an alternative treatment be found and offered to a prized breeding bitch.

In a few open cases the condition can be treated by a strong drug (this causes the uterus to contract) or by flushing the fluid away using a catheter. In closed cases an incision can be made in the uterus.

I personally have knowledge of this treatment, the need for which which arose following the mating of a young bitch at eighteen months. All went well until the significant five-week period after the season when this bitch quite suddenly discharged reddish-brown pus. After many deliberations, she was given a series of ten injections over a five-day period plus antibiotics, the object being to cause uterine contractions and flush out infection. At the time we could not tell if the treatment had been successful. This needed to be assessed at the next season when the cervix re-opened since the condition could have recurred. Luckily for me it did not, and the bitch did go on to have a litter of puppies. It was thought that she had initially conceived but that the early growing puppies had succumbed to infection. The treatment described was pioneered in the USA when forty bitches were treated with a strong drug, thirty-three successfully. In the seven remaining cases, there were valid reasons for failure such as heart conditions etc. Of the thirty-three bitches, fourteen were mated, with nine successfully producing litters.

SEBACEOUS ADENITIS

This skin disease does affect the Samoyed as well as some other breeds. It is a source of discomfort and has implications for a breeding programme.
Signs and Symptoms: In the mildest form, scaling may begin to be seen on the head and body. Initially, there may not be any coat loss, but the coat becomes dry. In more advanced cases, there will be serious coat loss, sometimes across the whole body. The skin might appear to be red and inflamed. This could be due to the disease itself or a secondary infection.
Secondary Infection: An unpleasant odour will be detected. The itchiness of the condition will bring about scratching and biting of the body by the dog. Unfortunately some bacteria are resistant to antibiotics. The sebaceous glands produce a fatty secretion which lubricates hairs, and they are responsible for normal gloss and coat production. The disease in the Samoyed breed damages these glands.
Action: Sebaceous adenitis can be diagnosed from a biopsy (skin scraping) by a vet. However, a breed survey has suggested that this biopsy can show as negative. Consult with your vet for treatment. The shampoo Korrect and moisturizer Humlac have proved to be successful.

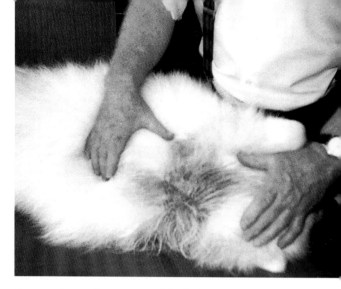

Samoyeds can be prone to skin irritations.

SKIN CONDITIONS

A very complex area. Since there can be many causes, diagnosis is often difficult. Sadly this problem does arise in the Samoyed breed. It is thought that chronic dermatitis can be caused by diet, an allergy to dust or antibiotics, a parasite, or feeding too much protein e.g. tripe alone. A skin test should discover the cause of the allergy which can present as hotspots, wet eczema, bald patches or scaling. I have seen two quite severe cases, one resulting in extensive hair loss and an eczema-like rash. Most veterinary schools do have a specialized dermatology department and, in perplexing cases, it would be worth discussing with your vet a referral to one of them. Homoeopathethic treatments are now also available as an alternative.

STREPTOCOCCAL INFECTION

Generally occurs in females and is a disease of the reproductive organs which prevents conception and can lead to young puppies being absorbed. In addition, puppies might be born healthy but become infected through their mother's milk resulting in 'fading puppy syndrome'. Reproductive organs of dogs born to such an affected litter can be infected. Any dog mated to an affected bitch can become a carrier within two days.

Action: Seek advice from your vet. A vaginal swab will establish whether infection is present. Antibiotics can be used.

Note: It is always sound practice to have a vaginal swab taken when a bitch comes into season; then if necessary she can be treated quickly. She should be removed from the company of any other dogs, and the kennels should be disinfected.

SWALLOWING FOREIGN OBJECTS
Young puppies unfortunately do act like vacuum cleaners picking up all sorts of objects both in the garden and the home. Any object which could be considered unsafe and could be ripped apart, such as rubber toys, socks and towels, should be removed. Do not feed your Samoyed chicken bones or anything brittle which could splinter in the stomach and pierce the stomach wall.

Action: Should you suspect an object could have been swallowed, consult your vet. Signs are excessive thirst, apathy and lack of appetite.

VACCINATIONS
Vaccine stimulates the body to produce antibodies. Young puppies are given an injection to protect them against the five major infectious diseases from which they might suffer. These are:

Canine Distemper
Signs and symptoms: High temperature, vomiting and diarrhoea, coughing, fits, twitching and paralysis. The foot pads and nose tend to thicken and peel, hence the common-known name 'hard pad'.

Action: After contacting the vet do not take the dog into the waiting room of the surgery. Dogs can recover but there can be damage to the nervous system.

Infectious Canine Hepatitis
Signs and symptoms: High temperature, vomiting and diarrhoea, abdominal pains, dehydration. The acute form is known as Rubarth's Disease.

Action: After contacting the vet, try to keep the dog isolated. A dog which has recovered may well be left with a blue clouding of the eye.

Leptospirosis
There are two types. Leptospira icterohaemorrhagiae is carried by rats and is a serious condition. Dogs can be infected by rat urine on the ground. Leptospira canicola is sometimes known as Lamp-post Disease and can be picked up by dogs sniffing urine from such an object.

Signs and symptoms: High temperature, severe thirst, increased urination, jaundice, diarrhoea containing blood, ulcerated mouth, coated tongue and persistent vomiting. Infection can be passed on to humans.

Action: May need a laboratory test for diagnosis. Dogs which recover should be kept in the same kennel area for six months.

Canine Parvovirus
There are two types. Canine Parvovirus Myocarditis occurs when a dam has not been vaccinated. She will have no protection to pass on to her puppies, so seemingly healthy puppies can collapse and die at around 4 to 10 weeks when their heart muscles are weakened. The second type is intestinal, affecting puppies

of four weeks and upwards, right into the dog's old age.

Signs and symptoms: Depression, vomiting, abdominal pain, refusal of food and water, diarrhoea containing blood.

Action: After contacting the vet it is important to try to isolate the dog. Dogs who survive can recover quite rapidly. With badly affected puppies, however, growth may be stunted and they may be lacking in hair for some time.

Kennel Cough (Infectious Canine Tracheo-bronchitis)

This usually occurs where large numbers of dogs are kennelled or gathered together, hence the name. Infection is airborne.

Signs and symptoms: Harsh coughing sound as if a dog has a bone stuck in the throat.

Action: After contacting the vet, do not allow contact with any other dogs – and do not go into the vet's waiting room. This condition tends not to be life-threatening but it can sometimes reoccur due to stress or over-exercise.

VON WILLEBRAND'S DISEASE

A bloodclotting disorder. Thankfully only an odd case has been diagnosed in Samoyeds in the UK.

WORMS

ENDOPARASITES (parasites which live inside the body)

There are two main types: Roundworm *Toxocara Canis*. This is thin and has a spaghetti-like appearance. Tapeworm *Dipylidium Caninum*. This has a segmented or rice-grain appearance. Both can cause illness in dogs but the roundworm Toxocara can cause illness in children as well. Roundworms are sticky and are passed in the stools of animals, making it easy for other dogs to pick them up when sniffing the ground. They can also be transmitted to puppies at birth. Tapeworm will pass through different species before re-ingestion in dogs. A heavy infestation of worms can weaken the dog's immunity and lead to other serious health problems.

There are many effective worming preparations. Take veterinary advice. Puppies need to be wormed monthly up to six months of age and then, throughout their adult life, twice a year. Worming is just part of being a responsible Samoyed owner.

NATURAL REMEDIES

There are now a number of veterinary practices which specialize in the use of homoeopathy for the treatment of animals. This is a natural healing process and stimulates the body's natural forces of recovery, concentrating on the animal not the disease. An excellent and informative booklet, *Homeopathy for Pets,* can be obtained from either a chemist or a health shop.

There are some excellent daily supplements, such as:

Garlic: A natural antiseptic which can be used to protect against infection and helps protect against coughs, catarrh and diarrhoea. Also liquid garlic can be used for bad-breath problems, cuts and bites.

Cod Liver Oil Capsules: Contain vitamins A and D. They help with stiffness in older dogs and are invaluable for pregnant bitches.

Seaweed Tablets: Help with pigment density and where coats are poor.

I acknowledge the help given by my veterinarian Richard Venables MRCVS with this chapter.

11 BREEDING A LITTER

hy would you want to breed? This is the question I invariably ask. Breeding is a complex business if undertaken properly, requiring careful thought and a degree of knowledge on the subject.

APPRAISING THE SITUATION
Many people think that just because they own a bitch she should be bred from and that a litter of puppies would be good for her. This is not necessarily the case. I consider that we all carry a huge responsibility towards our lovely breed and we should look to preserve the very highest qualities, passing these on to future generations, rather than passing on inferior specimens. It is a sad fact that these days, many thousand of dogs have to be put down as they are unwanted. Stop and think whether you would or might add to this problem. It is not unknown for a buyer no longer to want their puppy after nine months and refer it back to you. Believe me, it really does happen and you have a duty to either take that youngster back or find it another home. Rearing a litter is extremely hard if you are to look after the mother and puppies properly. It is difficult to imagine the work entailed.

CHOOSING A STUD DOG
I have in the past, received telephone calls from owners asking for their male Samoyed to be used at stud to any Samoyed bitch. Tact and patience are required when handling a call of this nature. I tend to turn the question around by asking why anyone should wish to use that dog when some simple enquiries would put them in touch with the best dogs in the country. Callers such as this tend only to be interested in making money out of their dog and are not interested in the breed as such.

It is certainly much more usual to receive enquiries from someone who wishes to mate a bitch. I then enquire how the bitch is bred, making reference to the pedigree. Should the pedigree not contain, in my opinion, any dogs of worth, the enquiry is still not rejected out of hand and I arrange for the bitch to be seen either by myself or by a breed specialist living nearby. The bitch may very well be stunning, but it is my experience that most turn out to be

Breeding a litter can be very rewarding, but careful thought and planning must go into the enterprise.

mediocre. Faced with a problem of a 'mediocre' bitch, what is to be done? It is a dilemma, but there are different ways of dealing with the situation.

My own way is to try and persuade the owner of the bitch to come to terms with the fact that no matter how good the stud dog is, subsequent puppies produced will in all probability be of inferior worth, with the possibility of the odd good one. I advise that such a bitch should be kept as a pet, but if the person concerned is really serious about breeding, then I advise that they purchase another puppy of better breeding which would give a solid building foundation. I am happy to report that most people do follow this advice. The other argument is to go

ahead with using the 'good' stud dog, since the owner may very well be intent on mating and using any dog at any cost. Although I am not in favour, it does occur.

Let us assume, therefore, that you do have a sound, well-bred bitch, which you want to mate. Which dog do you choose to put her to? Even if a dog is much admired, it might not be the right one for your own bitch. There are three types of breeding strategies which need to be considered at this stage.

TYPES OF BREEDING

In breeding
This is most difficult and is not to be

recommended without knowledge and experience. Smaller breeds tend mostly to follow this route. The danger is a 'doubling up' on faults and it can affect temperament. Examples: Mother to son, brother to sister, father to daughter matings.

Line breeding
This is usually the best way forward wherever possible. Again, there is a need for a considerable amount of breeding knowledge and study of pedigrees. Example: Grandfather to granddaughter mating.

Outcrossing
Sometimes used by breeders to introduce new blood lines and vigour. It occurs where there are no blood relations on either side of the pedigree. Again, a certain amount of experience is required. It is always good practice to seek advice from your bitch's breeder if she has been obtained from reputable stock.

SELECTING THE RIGHT DOG
Before making a decision, assess and think through the salient points. Make an honest assessment of your own bitch to the best of your ability. Look at her virtues and her faults. If the dog you have in mind has similar faults, you will only 'double up' on these faults. If you should decide to line breed, breed to the Standard, using a dog of suitable and similar type. Should you decide to outcross, you may not know or be aware of faults or gene problems in a particular line.

If the dog you are considering has already been used at stud, check to see what the puppies are like that he has previously thrown. A good choice of an outcross could be of enormous benefit, bringing together fresh bloodlines and substance. Do remember to breed back into your own lines if outcrossing in order to maintain type and quality. Even if you personally dislike the owner of a stud dog, their dog may still be right for you and you should not let this stand in your way. It is especially important with the Samoyed breed to preserve head quality. Once this is lost, it is difficult to regain. Remember, you are aiming for quality, substance and soundness. When you finally have found the dog who you hope will fulfil expectations, it will be useful to check the HD scores on both dog and bitch.

THE SEASON
If a bitch is mentally and physically mature enough, the best time to consider mating is at around 18 months to 2 years. Most bitches come into season around every seven months but some can be erratic. In some cases there is nothing you can do but to be patient and wait. The first real sign that a bitch is in season will be when you see her drop bright red spots on the floor from her vulva. Get a tissue and examine her vulva; you will see it gradually become bigger. She might attract but she will not normally mate with dogs during these early days. When the blood colour turns to straw the vulva will become really enlarged and the bitch will accept the male.

GOOD MATING INDICATIONS
The real key to mating on the right day is to know when a bitch is going to ovulate and to mate her two days later. The usual time for a bitch to be mated is normally the tenth or twelfth day into her season. There are always going to be exceptions

to the rule and it has been known for a bitch to ovulate as early as the fifth day and sometimes as late as the thirtieth day. One of the best ways of knowing when a bitch is ready to be mated is when you see her 'turning her tail', i.e. turning her tail to one side in order to receive the dog. Even if you own two bitches, it is quite common to see the bitch in season stand for the other bitch this way. Another indication is by means of a smear test which can be taken by your vet. A swab is taken from the vagina. When looked at under the microscope, if the bitch is ready for mating, the cells can be seen to change to an octagonal shape. This method of identifying correct timing is especially useful where a bitch has to travel a long distance to a stud dog.

MATING

When a bitch is eventually mated to the dog, the muscles in her vagina contract. This prevents the dog's penis from being withdrawn and is known as a tie. The dog will lift his leg over the back of a bitch. It is sometimes necessary for the dog to be helped with this so that the dog and bitch are back to back. The tie can last a few minutes or for as long as an hour. It is useful at this stage to glance at your watch in order to ascertain how long the tie lasts. After the dog and bitch pull apart, try and keep the bitch quiet by holding her down and gently rubbing her tummy. She will be highly excited and happy. If at all possible, try and repeat the mating again within the next couple of days. A bitch may be referred to as infertile but it could be she is not at all, she has just been mated at the wrong time.

DIFFICULT MATINGS

Matings themselves can be extremely easy or just very difficult. Marion Keyte-Perry always felt that dogs and bitches should be attracted to each other and she would never allow a forced mating. There are also numerous reasons why a dog and bitch might not mate together:

1. Bitch not fully in season and not ready to accept the dog.
2. The bitch was 'gone past' her season and the vulva decreased in size.
3. Sometimes if a bitch is taken and left with a stud dog in strange surroundings, the stress can delay ovulation.
4. Use of inexperienced maiden dog.
5. Putting together a maiden bitch and inexperienced maiden dog.
6. In a maiden bitch, there can be a problem with a stricture in the hymen which can prevent mating. Your vet should be able to help.
7. A dog may not be attracted to a bitch; he may be selective, mating with some bitches not others.
8. A bitch could have a vaginal infection and not want a dog to mate her.

FALSE PREGNANCY

This can happen when a bitch fails to conceive or even when she has not been mated. Around seventy-five days after a season the bitch can appear as if she is pregnant. Her teats will enlarge and she produces milk. She will possibly pant and start scrabbling about. She might even start to carry toys about as if she were carrying a puppy. Do not be too concerned, because in the wild such a bitch would become a foster mother. Speak with your vet.

CONCEIVING

A dog which has poor-quality sperm may very well produce sperm which does not live long enough.

STUD FEES

This needs to be agreed before mating takes place. If a bitch does fail to conceive, invariably a breeder will offer a repeat mating at the bitch's next season. Fees vary considerably. Top dogs can command large fees. Two-thirds the price of a puppy would be a general guide.

Well – I said it was a complex business but, despite all the foregoing, given a good brood bitch and an acceptable stud dog, matings and subsequent litters can and do work out like clockwork, producing healthy litters of puppies.

IS YOUR BITCH IN WHELP?

Now that your bitch has been successfully mated, the big question is whether or not she is in whelp. There are usually two early ways of finding this out, but not until the bitch is at least 28 days into her pregnancy. Firstly, your vet should be able to tell by examination. Puppies at this stage will feel like a string of beads spaced along the horns of the uterus. Sometimes with larger bitches, there can be some difficulty in feeling since the horns can be high inside the rib cage. Secondly, the bitch can be scanned using ultrasound. This measures heart-beats and growth rate of puppies and can be repeated if required as the pregnancy progresses.

This is entirely different to an X-ray because it causes no harm to the developing puppies. It will also detect any problems a puppy might be experiencing or, indeed, show if any puppies have died. Examine the teats on your bitch. You should find, if she is in whelp, that they are becoming pinker and larger. As far as food is concerned, she will start to become fussy or even quite ravenous. Her daily exercise must be kept up in order to keep her fit and strong enough to cope with the demands of labour.

CARE OF THE PREGNANT BITCH

Food needs to be gradually increased from the fourth week into pregnancy. No sooner, because the pups are tiny. If the bitch is fed on commercial food there will be no need for any supplements but raspberry tablets can be given in order to make whelping easier. The diet should be gradually increased, feeding in small amounts.

At eight weeks into the pregnancy the bitch should now be receiving her normal amount of food plus another half. Do not overfeed, making the bitch weighty, because this might hinder the whelping. Feed such things as chicken, fish, meat, eggs and cheese as well as normal biscuit. Introduce fresh vegetables and cereal and a drink of milk. Plenty of fresh water should be always in place. It could be that around the middle of the pregnancy, morning sickness might develop, with the bitch throwing up a frothy substance. This stage does not normally last very long.

Coat may well now start to come away round the teats. Another good pointer that the bitch is pregnant is that following the thirty-fifth day a discharge of white mucus can sometimes be seen coming from the vagina. If the bitch is pregnant, she will by now be looking really well and be in full bloom due to hormonal increases. You should discuss with your vet the date you suspect the puppies to be due. An average pregnancy lasts for 63 days. Some tend to whelp early but there could be variations from as much as 58 to 72 days. This is because the bitch can release eggs from the ovary which are still immature, so they may have to wait up to a couple of days to be fertilised. The dog's sperm may also live inside the bitch for up to ten days. If after 63 days, nothing seems to be happening, contact your vet. There is absolutely no need to be alarmed as long as she is still eating and looks comfortable enough.

PREPARATIONS FOR WHELPING
After the mating you need to decide where you want your bitch to have her puppies in your home. It is essential that somewhere quiet is chosen. Many people make use of a spare bedroom. A room adjoining the kitchen is ideal. If a garden shed is to be used it should be near the house, clean and warm.

An adequate whelping box should be made or purchased. Commercial ones are now available but most people tend to make their own. If you do decide to do this, you must make sure that there is sufficient room. At the very minimum it should be four feet square. There should be a rail four to six inches above the floor of the box so that the bitch does not lie on her puppies. There should be some sort of opening at the front so that as the pups grow older, they can come out: a hinge, or two pieces of wood slotted into a groove on either side of the box, can prove to be really useful. There are varying opinions as to whether the box should be covered or not. Mostly they are not. It is possible to make a whelping box from extra heavy-duty cardboard such as TV packaging. The advantage is that this can be replaced as often as necessary and will not collect germs. I have seen this used.

A modern whelping box.

The floor needs to be solid and can be covered with different materials. Newspaper on its own is not recommended for Samoyed puppies since the print will rub off and make the puppies grey. Wallpaper lining paper is ideal. This needs to be topped with fleecy dog-bedding which will allow urine to pass through. This is marvellous to use because, besides being warm and comfortable for the puppies, it can be easily washed in the washing machine. I advise keeping at least two lots of this bedding and to interchange them.

Allow the bitch into the whelping box long before the puppies are born to get her used to it. Keep a careful watch to make sure that she does not slope off into the garden and start digging a hole for herself. I had one pregnant bitch who disappeared on me. I found her quite black and covered with soil inside a large hole she had dug into the earth directly underneath her kennel.

HEATING
You must ensure that the newborn puppies will be kept warm, since cold can be life-threatening. The temperature of the surrounding area following birth should initially be about 80 degrees Fahrenheit. It is obviously ideal if there is a radiator in the room and an overhead infra-red lamp. Use of these will vary according to weather and season. The infra-red 'pig lamp' is still used but there are disadvantages and it is becoming rapidly outdated because the heat from it is directed to a spot on the centre of the whelping box and therefore there is little side heat. If any water comes in contact with this suspended lamp, it will shatter into small fragments, becoming totally dangerous both to the bitch and litter.

An electric heating pad which can be placed under the fleecy dog-bedding is now much used in place of the pig lamp by some breeders. Only half the floor space needs to be covered. The bitch will not wish to lie on this because she will become too hot. You must also ensure that the electric cord goes out through a hole at the rear or side of the box and is well clear of the bitch, for obvious safety reasons and to prevent chewing.

ESSENTIAL ITEMS
You will need to have close at hand the following items: sterilised scissors, thermometer, towels, hot-water bottle and small cardboard box, supply of refuse bags for soiled items, iodine, notebook and pen, scales to weigh puppies, eyedropper, small feeding bottle, teats, milk formula, cotton wool (cotton), a sterilising liquid.

THE BIRTH
It is a good idea to take the temperature of a pregnant bitch from the 57th day onwards by inserting a clinical thermometer into her rectum. Her normal temperature will be 101.5 degrees Fahrenheit (33.8 degrees C). However, twenty-four hours before the puppies are due, the hormonal changes will cause the temperature to drop.

The bitch will start to become very restless, starting to dig, scrabble about, scratch the floor and walls and shred up newspaper. She is actually attempting to nestmake and this can go on for up to 12 hours or so. She will eventually go off her food and start to puff and pant. You must monitor your bitch closely now and keep any other animals away from her. Having encouraged your bitch to sit in her whelping box, sit with her. You will

*A contented litter
will suckle contentedly
from their mother.*

notice when she starts to strain, there will be intervals in between and it will not be long before her waters break. The fluid coming away will be green or dark brownish, the colour of the placenta or afterbirth. Try and keep the whelping box as clean as possible by renewing the paper under your bitch or even using an absorbent pad.

Keep reassuring your bitch by talking to her quietly. You will notice the contractions increasing and the bitch starting to push. Check for the puppy arriving. Sometimes a bitch will stand up to drop a puppy so it is essential that there is something soft placed in the whelping box to cushion the puppy's fall. More often the puppy will just slide out head first while the bitch is in a sitting position. The puppy should appear in a bag or sack which is attached by a cord to the afterbirth. Although the bitch may break this afterbirth herself, you need to be standing by to make a cut with the sterilised scissors approximately one inch away from the puppy if necessary. Dot the end of the cord with iodine.

It is essential to get the puppy out of the bag as soon as possible. Again, this is something that the bitch herself might do but if it is her first litter she may be overwhelmed by it all and not really understand what is going on. Using the clean, dry towels, quickly rub and dry the newborn puppy. Ensure that the nose and mouth are free from mucus and that the puppy is breathing. If a puppy appears to be lifeless, do not give up. Clear the airways and give the puppy a hard slap and swing downwards for some minutes, hoping that it will gasp for air. Once the puppy is breathing and towelled dry, give it to the mother.

She will start to lick it furiously. Then place the puppy on a teat. Her milk will now start to flow. It is useful at this stage to have on hand another small box containing a hot-water bottle wrapped in a towel. Keep the box where it can be seen by the mother in the whelping box but place the newborn puppy in here after a period of time to enable the bitch to concentrate on producing the next puppy. The puppy will be warm and out of harm's way. Every so often place the puppy back on a teat. This suckling action tends to bring about the next contraction. As each puppy arrives, check its weight and afterbirth.

THE AFTERBIRTHS
It is acceptable for the bitch to eat up to two afterbirths because the placenta does contain nourishment which stimulates milk. If an afterbirth is retained, an injection from the vet will get rid of it,

because a retained afterbirth can be dangerous. The times between puppies arriving vary enormously. Some bitches have them like shelling peas, dropping one every half an hour or so, but it is not often you can be so lucky. There can be gaps of two or up to four hours between puppies. Do not forget to give the bitch a drink of water and let her out into the garden to empty her bladder – but watch her carefully in case she drops another puppy.

BIRTH COMPLICATIONS

If a bitch strains for more than two hours without producing a puppy, contact your vet. It may be that you need to take her to the surgery. If that is the case, any pups already born should also be taken to the surgery in their small cardboard box containing the hot-water bottle wrapped in a towel.

Some bitches suffer inertia. This can also occur with overweight or older bitches. The bitch appears to be resting and does not strain. She will probably need to have a Caesarean section.

Secondary inertia can also occur when a bitch has been straining for a long time or she has a large litter. The womb just gets tired and gives up. An injection of oxytocin will probably help here. A car ride to the vet's can quite often help a bitch to drop a puppy. Twice it has been my experience for a puppy to be dropped by a bitch, in the dark, in a crate in the back of a car. Double-check for this happening. On a dark winter's night, one puppy's life was only saved when squeaking noises where heard coming from the back of the car after the bitch had been removed.

Of course, a bitch may well have to have a Caesarean for other reasons, but there is no reason why she should not fully recover. A dead puppy blocking the uterus will stop everything. Sometimes puppies can be lost under anaesthetic, but do not worry about this unduly.

It is not uncommon to experience lactation problems following a Caesarean and I personally experienced this with one bitch. Again, allow the bitch to eat up the two placentas to assist with the flow of milk.

POST-WHELPING CARE

Let us hope that you now have a healthy, contented litter of puppies suckling away at Mum in the whelping box. Let Mum out into the garden. She will no doubt dash back in like a tornado. Give her a drink of milk or water, also a teaspoonful of dissolved glucose. Offer her a little food, possibly chicken.

One point to note is that you can never be sure when a bitch has finished whelping, so you should continue to keep watching her. I have been caught out twice with this. I had one bitch who produced a surprise puppy after eight hours. However, when finally all seems to be finished, clean up both the bitch and the whelping box. There will be a lot of staining on the bitch and it is a good idea to cut some of the coat away on her skirts. The vet will need to see your bitch again the following day and give her an injection to make her womb close down and to prevent any infection. Monitor the puppies closely for the next 48 hours, keeping away all visitors. An average Samoyed litter will contain six puppies. At birth, puppies can vary in weight from eight ounces to over one pound, fourteen ounces being a good average.

12 REARING THE LITTER

Now that all the stress of pregnancy and trauma of birth is over, the one-day-old puppies should look glossy and sleek and have a chubby look; when held up they should have little fat tummies. Body temperature will be 94-99 degrees Fahrenheit. Do not be complacent, however. You must still be alert to any other problems which may arise. Do keep any other dogs away from the puppies until at least three weeks of age, since bacteria and viruses can be transmitted even from the coats of healthy dogs.

THE FIRST WEEK
Hopefully, the puppies will be snuggled up to mum, but a careful check should be undertaken to ensure that each pup is actually suckling from a teat. A tip with any young pup who appears to be a slow starter, is to place honey on your fingertip, then transfer it to the bitch's

Now the hard work of rearing a litter begins.

teat. This will get glucose back into the system.

The pups should crawl about making a small humming noise, although sleeping for most of the time. They will be able to find their mother, but sometimes a young puppy will seem rejected or will be turfed out. There is usually a good reason for this but it is not always easy to understand. There might well be something fundamentally wrong with this youngster. Perhaps the puppy has been born with a heart defect or has a cleft palate, which is a split at the back of the mouth. At birth it could have picked up an infection or sustained an injury. It is easy enough to check for a cleft palate, by placing the little finger in the roof of the mouth. You must bear in mind that with any litter, it is inevitable that you may lose, at the very least, one puppy. Check each puppy's anus, since a pup can survive for some days without one, before eventually dying.

FADING PUPPY SYNDROME
Sometimes a puppy will stop feeding after a number of days and just die. The cause of this is still not fully understood.

Very occasionally, a bitch will fail to produce enough milk for her young. You must check the bitch's mammary glands. They should be enlarged and soft, not hard, lumpy or painful. If they are hard, it is probably mastitis, which is inflammation of the milk glands. Take direct action by telephoning for the vet and place hot wet towels on the glands.

Hungry puppies do tend to cry a lot and it may be that you need to supplement mum's milk. Smaller puppies tend to be pushed out by larger ones, especially with a large litter, so it is sometimes necessary to 'top up' these puppies using a milk replacer such as Whelpi. You should always have such products to hand and they should be purchased from a pet shop or the vet's prior to the birth. It is also a good idea to try and ensure that the smaller puppies get an adequate supply of mum's milk by lifting the larger, greedier ones off a teat and holding a smaller one in place for a period.

HAND FEEDING
If you do have a problem and a young puppy needs to be bottle-fed, this should be undertaken initially every two hours both day and night. This is a long, tiring and wearisome process. I can speak here from personal experience, having raised a litter in this way. My husband, Ray, and I devised a system whereby he would go to bed until 3.00 am. I would hand-feed the puppies until that time, when we would change over and I would go to bed and he would get up and feed the pups. That way we both got some sleep and we found that we were able to follow that routine for several days, exhausting as it was. Should a puppy fail to suckle while attempting to bottle-feed, depress the bottom of the teat in order to allow milk to be taken into the mouth. Gently stroke the throat to encourage the suckling action or stroke the muzzle on either side of the nose.

It is essential to be very, very careful, ensuring that no liquid gets into the lungs, since this can cause pneumonia. If milk comes down the nose, stop feeding. It is always apparent when young puppies are feeding because air bubbles can be seen passing through the bottle. Rotate the teat while the puppy sucks, since this seems to bleed air into both the teat and bottle.

Ray and I once spent almost three weeks bottle-feeding a puppy, who suckled intermittently. I had also taken the puppy to my vet's Labrador bitch who had a litter of puppies, but he would not suckle from her either. Eventually this puppy did become strong enough to feed off his own mother. Today, no-one would dream what a perilous start to life this young dog had. We never did find out what was wrong. He is now a strong, healthy and magnificent dog who went on to become Champion Naduska Double Oh Seven, and is our testimony to dedication and perseverance.

I have found from personal experience that, although various feeders can be freely obtained, a premature-baby bottle with teat and valve is by far the easiest to use. Getting a hole in the teat is a common problem. Be very careful and just snick a tiny hole with a pair of small, fine, sterilised scissors, so that when the bottle is pointed down, a slow drip results. Too small a hole means that the puppy will exhaust itself getting next to nothing, while too large a hole will mean the milk may go down into the lungs. Some people will also resort to using a syringe or eye-dropper, but I am wary of these methods since invariably milk will get into the lungs. Hygiene is all-important too. All feeding equipment should be sterilised between feeds and sterilising liquid is ideal for this.

THE PUPPY'S BOWELS AND BLADDER

After hand-feeding the puppies, rub the tummy gently with a warm cottonwool ball and rub the anus with damp cottonwool. This will stimulate the puppy both to urinate and pass a motion. Any puppies with constipation should also be treated the same.

Greedy puppies can develop diarrhoea and develop wind. Lectade, a glucose supplement, can be obtained from the vet for diarrhoea. This is additionally useful as a source of rapid energy supply to any weak puppies. Do not be alarmed when you see Mum cleaning up after her puppies, this is perfectly normal.

THE POST-WHELPING MOTHER

Have a look at the bitch's vulva. This will become smaller. It is also normal to see a small amount of blood, but if there is any obnoxious discharge, contact the vet. Mum should be pampered and for the first few days she should be given milky drinks, rice puddings, etc. Eventually, she will become quite ravenous and should be given plenty of such things as meat, chicken and fish. She will not want to leave her puppies and it may be necessary to be extremely firm with her to make her go out into the garden to do her jobs – then she will dash back. Always ensure that dewclaws on the puppies are removed by the vet in consultation with him at around three days.

THE SECOND WEEK

You will be amazed at how quickly the puppies will grow. When first born, their pigmentation is always mostly pink but, within days, dark spots will appear which eventually join up to produce the black nose, black eye-rims and black pigmentation around the mouth. The puppies will open their eyes at about seven to ten days. Their birthweight will double in eight to ten days. Continue to weigh and record your findings so that failing puppies can be spotted.

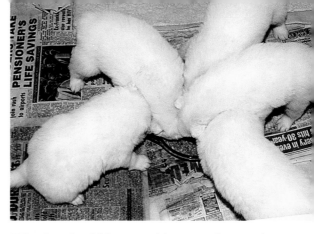

INITIAL SOCIALISATION

As the puppies grow larger, the temperature in the whelping room should be lowered. The puppies will be crawling about and by three weeks will really be on the move and will be standing. They will become inquisitive. Baby teeth will also appear at this stage.

Twenty-one days is a very crucial land-mark for the socialisation of young puppies and their involvement with humans. Puppies who do not have human contact between this and another crucial time, the forty-second day, can be difficult and unresponsive. This can very easily apply to puppies brought up in an outside shed who do not make human contact.

The mother will now leave the puppies frequently to seek some peace. It is essential that the puppies should now be exposed to noisy and normal living situations if they are to become well-balanced. Get out the vacuum cleaner, turn on the TV, bang a few pots and pans and expose the puppies to children. I sometimes carry young puppies outside in my arms so that they can experience street and road noises. With a summer litter puppies can be sometimes be placed in a pen in the garden – but make sure it is in shade, because the youngsters have difficulty with strong light.

WEANING

At three to four weeks of age, the puppies need to be weaned from their mother. Nowadays, breeders have enormous choice about this and about diet. Raw meat used to be the traditional food of the breed and this would require a calcium supplement. It may be that you might choose to continue with this method. If this is the case, on the first

Weaning should be started between three and four weeks.

day of weaning, cut off a small cube of beef. Holding it in the left hand, scrape off the meat onto a board with your right hand, or the other way round if you are left-handed. Feed to each puppy separately by popping the meat into its mouth with your fingers.

On the third day, provide two similar meat meals, one in the morning and one in the evening. On the fifth day, add to the meat meals a small drink of milk; there are some excellent milk preparations on the market which can be bought from your vet, pet shops or shows. Do not use cow's milk as this cannot be digested by puppies at this stage.

The puppies will paddle all over this meal and then lick each other. It is messy but they have to learn how to take their new food. Milk can be sweetened with a little honey. On the seventh day, provide another milky meal, making four meals in all: meat for breakfast and tea, milk for lunch and supper.

Increase all quantities gradually and at five weeks add some crumbled Farley's rusks to the milk. The meat can now be minced or finely cut and some puppy meal or crumbled cereal added to it. Raw egg and milk, baked custard or porridge can now take the place of one of the milk meals. Give a little calcium supplement daily. By eight weeks each puppy should be having half-a-pound of meat per day.

A second choice for puppy rearing can now be made from any number of excellent commercial preparations which are available.

I myself have graduated from the traditional method to using a commercial puppy porridge/cereal which the puppies love and which is so much easier to feed. When using a commercial preparation, carefully follow instructions on the feeding charts, upgrading the preparations at the recommended age. Start the puppies off by gently pushing their faces and mouths into the dish. It is desirable to feed all the puppies using separate dishes. That way, you will control the feeding and ensure that all puppies get the same amount of food. With a large litter of, say, eight puppies, feed four at a time because some will be slow eaters while others will gobble their food and run to the next dish. A new puppy feeder has just come on to the market. It is joined up with four feeding compartments on either side. This should prove invaluable.

It is also useful to be aware that some very maternal bitches will regurgitate food for their puppies. They are not being sick. If this happens, puppies will leap up to mum's mouth and we did have one bitch who had part of her tongue nicked away by sharp puppy teeth. Mum's milk supply and protein intake should be gradually reduced and the puppies removed from her more frequently. She will still have some milk and will not completely stop producing until all of the puppies are gone.

Worm the puppies at three to four weeks with a worming preparation obtained and prescribed by the vet. The puppies should develop their hearing now and personalities will develop.

THE FIFTH WEEK
The pups will now be very active. Any visitors will be asked to remove their shoes and disinfect their hands before handling the puppies. It is a good idea to place newspapers by the door to encourage the pups to go to the door when they need to empty out. Praise the puppies for this.

An evenly matched litter of eight puppies.

The puppies become increasingly energetic and inquisitive, and much time can be spent 'puppy watching'.

THE SIXTH WEEK

The puppies will now be even more energetic. They will need one-to-one handling. Watch mum and the puppies at play since they will now become adventurous and more rough.

LEAVING HOME

By seven or eight weeks, the puppies should all be eating normally and should be healthy and lively and ready to go to their new homes. Hopefully, prospective purchasers will have been vetted thoroughly. I tend to try and put people off, knowing full well if they are really keen to have a puppy, nothing in the world will put them off. If you are at all doubtful, hang on to the puppy, since other people will come along. You must always act responsibly and be prepared to have the puppy or older dog back if circumstances change or the new owners feel unable to look after it. The puppies' mother will not be too unhappy that they have gone, since she will now have some peace and more attention to herself.

New owners should be given a number of articles and I usually make up a complete pack to contain the following:

- A copy of the puppy's pedigree.
- Kennel Club Registration Certificate. (Take time to explain this document and advise that a transfer into the purchaser's name should be undertaken.)
- Copy of any insurance cover.
- A Diet Sheet. Give a sample or small supply of the food used and the names of suggested suppliers. I sometimes also purchase a small rounded puppy-collar since these are not always easy to obtain and, occasionally, a brush and comb. New owners should be shown how to groom their puppy before they leave, and should be told that you are always available by phone at any hour of the day or night should problems arise. They should be advised that young puppies are made of water and cannot properly control their functions until at least 12 weeks.

126

At eight weeks of age, it is time for the puppies to go to their new homes.

Sometimes puppy bitches can go on what is called Breeding terms. If this happens, it is essential that a Breeding Terms Agreement is signed by both parties. But always be very careful about selling on Breeding terms.

Ask people to keep in touch and they usually will. At Christmas-time it is very fulfilling to receive cards and photos of the growing Samoyed from your purchasers. Remember the golden rule: it is essential to place a puppy in a happy and caring environment.

127

13 THE SAMOYED IN BRITAIN

After the Second World War the era of the large kennels had disappeared. Instead kennels became smaller and much more numerous. Ordinary people, not just those living in mansions, found that they were able to keep a small number of dogs for pet or show and new breeders came to prominence. Irene Ashfield was the daughter of Mrs D. L. Perry and took over the reins of the world-renowned Kobe Kennel. Rose Lewis purchased a foundation bitch from Mrs Westcott for her Snowcryst Kennels which she made up to Champion. This was Ch.

Snowland Marda, the first Samoyed to go Best Bitch All Breeds in Samoyeds. From there the Snowcryst kennel gained momentum with many dogs being exported to Holland.

POST-WAR SUCCESSES

Ivor Munday bought his first Samoyed, Snowfire Gem, in 1949 purely as a pet. It was discovered that she possessed her good breeding from the Kobe line. In 1951 Ivor mated her to a dog registered as Sergi of Gwyneira, who himself was mainly Kobe/Snowland breeding. This mating produced a dog he called Alaskan

Betty Cobby (second left) with fellow fanciers at a show after the Second World War.

Snowstorm, who became the first Samoyed in Wales to win Best In Show (All Breeds) under one of the greatest all-rounders of the time, Leo Wilson. All this occurred in the days before Ivor obtained his Samovar affix. Later, another dog bred by Ivor and owned by Chrissy Andrews, Ch. Samovar Will O'Wisp, won the CC at Crufts three years in succession. Ivor then continued to breed under the Samovar affix and, in conjunction with Rose Lewis, produced a number of English and International Champions. He became an International Judge, judging in New Zealand, and is still on the Samoyed scene today.

In 1956, Robin Lings obtained his first two Samoyeds. These were Goldcloud Queen Armada and Goldcloud Leading Light, which had been left in a kennel by passing gypsies. They were of the very old Icefloe breeding and good specimens. From there Robin developed his own Delmonte line which really took off. He was able to boast of no less than 40 wins alone at Crufts in the years that he exhibited there.

Mr W. E. Lloyd, later to become a Secretary of the Samoyed Association, had the Tundra Kennels which were a force to be reckoned with, while Mrs Olive Howard of Wigan had the Snowpack Kennels. She produced Champions from Kobe stock and was to become the first President of the Northern Samoyed Society.

DARRYL OF TAMITSA
Phyllis Clarke and Ethel Hobson owned the Tamitsa kennels which produced lovely litters. Together they bred a number of English Champions. However, the most famous dog they bred was Darryl Of Tamitsa, who was to become an English and Australian Champion. Ethel relates the story of Darryl, sold at six weeks to Gloria Gittoes from Australia who was in England staying with Bunty Ross. He was shown by Gloria and made up to an English champion at nine months, being the youngest English champion in the breed. (The requirement for a further CC to be acquired after twelve months was introduced later.) Darryl was then sent out to Australia to await the return of his owner, Gloria. However, she married and did not return, hence Yvonne Sydenham-Clarke became the owner of this wonderful dog.

Mrs M. M. Ross, always called Bunty, in her era, produced one of the most successful kennels of Samoyeds, breeding

Int. Ch. Janet Janmayen exported to the USA by Sheila and Charles Duke.

many Sworddale Champions, all of whom were known for their lovely heads. Much stock was also sent out to the USA. There were fourteen Champions in all.

CONSOLIDATING LINES
The beginning of the 1950s saw the establishment of the Crownie Kennel founded by the now Judge John Hopkin QC consolidating on the earlier work of his parents, Muriel and Raymond Hopkin. The Hopkins actually purchased their first Samoyed, a dog puppy called Scaf, in 1943. He was from a Miss Hutchinson in Nottingham and was of Snowland/Arctic breeding. Their foundation bitch was Aura Of Silverfrost who was from Florrie Walter in Newcastle. She too was of Snowland/Arctic breeding. The kennel went on to produce many fine dogs known for their plush coats and good heads. Eight Champions were produced in all and Mrs Muriel Hopkin was to become a President of the Northern Samoyed Society for over twenty-five years.

1952 saw Margaret Wilcock purchase her first Samoyed, Snowpack Storm, from Olive Howard, although her late husband had previously acquired one. Storm already had a CC when he was bought and was only allowed to go on the understanding that he continued to be shown. He was, of course, and became the first Annecy Champion. Margaret is still showing, breeding and judging to date and there are no less than 27 English Champions bearing the Annecy affix and numerous ones overseas, taking the total to over 40. This kennel holds the post-war record for keeping most Champions at one time –

at one stage there were ten. These days, Annecy dogs are shown by Robin Newhouse and together they are an amazingly successful team. Margaret is now a Vice President of the Samoyed Owners and Breeders League.

Mrs Gladys Varney exhibited under the Carwood affix. In 1955 she was to breed Ch. Snowking of Carwood. Rex, as he was known, was bred from Snowqueen of Carwood ex Kim of Crownie and was to amass twenty-four CCs in his lifetime.

A NEW ERA
1962 saw the beginning of a new era in the breed. Eileen Danvers and her husband Tiny, as he was known, started breeding under the Fairvilla affix. They were widely respected and both held high office in the Samoyed Association; Eileen was the President twice and Tiny the Secretary. Together, they significantly carried the breed forward over a long period very ably, exporting stock abroad and successfully producing a Fairvilla type and 37 Champions. Their dogs were always noticeably of a steady temperament and I can still see Eileen in my mind's eye leaving a showground with six dogs, three leads being held in each hand. Not many could manage that today without the aid of a halti.

Terri Malabar was also well known for her Airebis kennel. She was to breed another most famous dog who was to set his stamp on the breed and who appears in many pedigrees today. Ch. Fairvilla Istvan of Airebis was bred from Ch. Snowfern of Carwood ex Ch. Demetrio of Kobe. He was owned by Eileen Danvers and went on to become an International Champion. He went Reserve Best in Show at Leeds

Championship Show in 1968 and Reserve Best in the Working Group at Crufts in 1969, only being beaten by the BIS winner.

The 60s saw the emergence of yet another very successful kennel of excellent type – Beryl and Geoff Grounds of the Whitewisp kennel. Again they were breeders of quality dogs from Kobe stock. They produced 13 Champions in all. Geoff Grounds was to become a President of the Samoyed Association and much later Beryl Grounds became President of the Samoyed Owners and Breeders League and the Breed Liaison Officer.

Betty Poole proudly flew the Golway flag. Around the same period, she exported to Sweden dogs which went on to do a great deal of winning in that country. Six Champions were bred, the most notable being Ch. Golway Mr

Ch. Fairvilla Snow Imp.

Chan. Betty was the President of the British Samoyed Club at the time of her sudden death.

Yet another kennel, held in high esteem in the late 1960s was Mr and Mrs John James's Crensa Kennel. John was the breeder of a dog who was to become the breed record holder of that period. He was Ch. Grenadier Of Crensa, born in 1969 from Ch. Fairvilla Istavan Of Airebis ex Venus of Crensa. He was to accrue no less than 43 CCs during his lifetime, being successfully shown and campaigned by John's second wife, Betty. This dog, known as Scot, was of the most gentle and loving disposition – an attribute he passed on to much of his progeny. Nine other Champions were also to emerge from this kennel.

GOOD LUCK OR GOOD JUDGEMENT?
It was noticeable that some people coming into the breed at this time immediately hit a winning streak and were enormously lucky both in the show ring and also with breeding stock. What must be taken into account is the fact that they were actually consolidating on the good breeding lines of the previous breeders.

At the beginning of the 1970s, without a doubt, the predominant kennels were Airebis, Annecy, Carwood, Crensa, Crownie, Delmonte, Golway, Fairvilla, Lealsam, Sarbesha, Snowmyth, Snowscene, Snowcryst, Samovar and Whitewisp.

Kiskas was also a kennel founded on the Crownie lines and this was the affix of Gerald and Kath Mitchell, who were later to become famous for being the pioneers of the Akita breed in the UK. During the 1970s Kath was the Secretary

Ch. Samovar Ice Crystal.

of the Northern Samoyed Society, and Gerald Chairman of the British Samoyed Club. They were both to become International Championship Show Judges. One of their most famous dogs was a dog they called Painter. He was acquired from breeders Tom and Joyce Stamp of the Karaholme kennel and was known as Kiskas Karaholme Cherokee. He went on to become a very famous Champion indeed in America. The story is that Bob and Dolly Ward, themselves authors of *The Complete Samoyed*, came over to Crufts in 1973. There, standing in seventh place in the Open dog class, was Painter. Immediately recognising the quality of this dog, they bought him. Thus Painter went off to the USA, where he proceeded to become an American Champion and stamped his mark on the breed over there. Incidentally the Mitchells owned a bitch, Owlie of Crownie, who won two CCs and

Ch. Naduska Grit Of Kiskas

Ch. Kiskas Silverstar Of Naduska.

132

seventeen reserve CCs. They also had three other Champions.

It is from the Mitchells' Kiskas kennel that we obtained our foundation bitch who was destined to become Ch. Kiskas Silverstar Of Naduska. Mated to Ch. Grenadier Of Crensa, she produced in her first litter Ch. Naduska Grit Of Kiskas who was bought and successfully campaigned by the Mitchells. Four other Champions were to come from Naduska.

Shirley Mann established the Sammymann kennels in South Wales and bred three Champions.

INTERNATIONAL CONNECTIONS
Around this time, another breeder emerged who was to become internationally famous. This was Betty Moody, who came to live in Oxford together with her husband who was in the US Army. She originally purchased from Eileen Danvers a Fairvilla bitch. This was the start of a tremendously successful showing and breeding programme. Betty, together with her sister, Wyn Collier, was able to make up and breed many Champions. Betty became Secretary of the British Samoyed Club for a short period before eventually returning to live in the United States. She successfully carried on her breeding programme there, as did her sister in the UK. As a result Novaskaya stock, and many Champions, can be found in most other parts of the world including New Zealand, Australia, Canada and Scandinavia. Betty has become an International Judge and also judged at Crufts.

Derek and Thelma Pont of the Samont kennel obtained a bitch who was to become Ch. Katrina Of Fairvilla, winning a Best Of Breed at Crufts. Derek and Thelma are both

Championship Judges, and breeding and exhibiting. They have bred a number of Champions, and Thelma is to judge at Crufts in 2001.

Still later came Chris McCrae exhibiting Samoyeds and Siberian Huskies under the Zoox affix, and Val Freer, now Secretary of the British Samoyed Club, commenced her showing career with yet another Fairvilla Champion, Fairvilla Kamelia, and took up the affix Nikara.

Neil and Elaine Banner bought stock and established themselves for a short period under the Nenetsky banner. There was also Donald Jackson, who had just acquired the Kazymir affix when, sadly, he suddenly died. All of the foregoing were to have valuable stock and themselves produce Champions. This line is carried on now by Eileen and Tiny's daughter, Angela Danvers-Smith under the Fairvilla Imperial affix – and still the Champions emerge.

In the North East the Lireva Kennels gained prominence with the two Averils – Averil Cawthera Senior and Young Averil Cawthera-Purdy. Averil Senior founded the kennel and much of the showing was done by 'young Averil' combining with Betty Cobby's Torvik breeding to produce Champion stock. Young Averil now co-ordinates the Kennel Club Junior Organisation and is a Kennel Club Accredited Trainer.

A FORTUITOUS MATING
Towards the end of the 1970s something quite remarkable happened that was to have enormous impact on the breed. Mr Jim Dougall of Eyemouth, Berwickshire, decided to mate his bitch, Samont Charmaine with Mr and Mrs Findley's Herondale Boris. On the face of it not an event out of the ordinary – but what was

133

Ch. Fairvilla Imperial Aga Khan.

produced out of that mating was spectacular, to say the least. On close examination of the pedigrees of both these dogs it is really not surprising that something special had to emerge. The blood lines are a magnificent collection, going back through Sworddale Champions, through Ch. Fairfax to Kobe, and include Ch. Fairvilla Katrina, Crensa, Snowland and Int. Ch. Fairvilla Istvan Of Airebis. Quite superb. The result of this mating was a litter which eventually produced no less than three Champions, which were exhibited under Jim Dougall's Hurkur affix. These were Jim's own bitch, Ch. Hurkur Hollyberry, the Golders' Ch. Hurkur Nicholas and Jim and Carole Hamilton's Ch. Hurkur Jingles, who was to become a legend in his own lifetime.

With Ch. Hurkur Jingles, the Hamiltons quickly established a line of their own and exhibited under the Zamoyski affix. In a short time they had produced a number of Champions, which is not surprising given the influence of this wonderful sire. They then obtained from Eileen Danvers a bitch who quickly was to become Ch. Fairvilla Silver Jewel. Mated to Ch.

Hurkur Jingles she produced a puppy who was bought by Carol Fox. This was Ch. Zamoyski Lucky Star Of Ostyak. Campaigned by Carol Fox, he became Breed Record Holder with 52 CCs.

TYPE AND QUALITY

The Samoyed story continued to gain momentum. There was a nucleus of dedicated enthusiasts, knowledgeable enough to build on solid foundations without losing type and quality. Val and Roly Miller's Mivisam kennel, started from Crensa stock, made up four Champions, and combined with Lesley Morgan to produce Ch. Snowmyth Mivara, now the breed bitch record holder. The Dobsons' Shimmaneke kennel founded on Whitewisp stock, went on to own another top winning dog, Ch. Hilsar Silver Shadow Of Shimmaneke, a Working Group winner bred by Hilary Breeze and Sarah Styles.

John and Pat Sharp's Karazoe kennel was built on Fairvilla and Samont lines. They were enormously successful, producing Champions both in the UK and in Europe. In the south of the country Pam and George Tyler's Tysam kennel and Pauline Caller's Silverfire kennel carried lines from both Airebis and Annecy and all produced Champions. John and Marie Ree's Reemack Samoyeds originated from Samont lines. They went on to breed their own Champions, and Ch. Reemack Katriona went on to win BOB at Crufts. It is impossible to mention all who were successful.

EARLY 1990S

Ray and Kay Pyecroft bought stock from Karazoe and developed their own Pykra lines and very quickly made up a number of Champions. Pat Hemmings

134

campaigned Ch. Aurora Borealis Of Samovar At Hemshire and had a long run of success. Lloyd and Penny Winger also had a run of success with Ch. Novaskaya Imry Lafay, a biscuit-shaded dog, who became another Crufts BOB winner. Ian Ross's lovely bitch Ch. Papagena Of Samovar charmed everybody, and the Sarnoushka kennel of Patsy Weller made up three Champions, while Ch. Nikitta Winter Breeze emerged for Gina Hounslow. Val Freer's Nikara Samoyeds were consistent winners, with Val quickly making up Ch. Nikara Kahoots, and Angela Danvers-Smith, who herself became President of the Samoyed Association, made up two Champions.

THE WAY FORWARD
Throughout the 1990s there was no stopping the relentless success of two major kennels, Annecy and Zamoyski. The Annecy Kennel is possibly the one that has been the longest in existence. Under Margaret Wilcox and Robin Newhouse, Champions continue to be produced – an amazing feat. The Annecy Kennel will hold the record in the UK for the number of Champions produced and owned. The Zamoyski Kennel of the Hamiltons continues to go from strength to strength, exporting winning stock to both Europe and the USA. Recently they lost Ch. Lucky Dexter Of Zamoyski at fourteen years of age. However, they were instrumental in breeding Ch. Zamoyski Lucky Casanova, known as Topper, from Ch. Pykra Spring Bear At Roybridge ex Ch. Zamoyski Lucky Melissa. Topper is owned by Bridget and Roy Enticott and shown by granddaughter Donna Fleming.

There seems to be a battle between two very successful top dogs – Ch.

Ch. Annecy's Sweet Surprise: A recent star from his prestigious kennel.

Ch. Lucky Dexter Of Zamoyski.

135

Zamoyski Lucky Casanova At Roybridge on 32 CCs and Pat Hemmings' Ch. Hemshire Snow Bear, known as Scruffy, on 23 CCs. These two dogs tend to alternate in taking top awards and both are Northern Samoyed Society Samoyeds of the Year. Occasionally both are beaten by Jebson's Ch. Novaskaya Zakrek Lafay who went BOB at Crufts in 1999. Shown infrequently, but of wonderful breed type, is Andrea Kirkwood's Ch. Diquest Levi Of Vandreem who went on to win BOB at Crufts in 2000 and came third in the Pastoral Group.

Of the top bitches, Cameron and Kirkwood's Ch. Vandreem Imperial Montana is much admired and was the Northern Samoyed Society's 'Samoyed of the year' in 1999. Kerri Main's Ch. Samont Vanya Of Aeylish continues to hold her own. An extremely attractive bitch, she had her portrait painted after a BOB win at Crufts a few years ago. These then are the latest keepers of the breed. The way forward lies here.

THE SHOW SCENE OF YESTERYEAR

Years ago, a popular way of travelling to shows was by train. Not everybody had cars and it was probably less tiring and more comfortable than sitting in endless traffic queues. However journeys to Scotland would take three days there and back, with the Show in between. Up until the 1950s, there was no Crufts qualification. Exhibitors merely entered like any other Championship show.

On arriving at the Championship show, the first thing exhibitors would do was 'make up' their own bench. It was, in effect, another competition to see who might have the most attractive bench. In those days there were no Kennel Club regulations in force imposing restrictions. Often there were to be found benches covered with red velvet, black and white satin, gold velvet and black satin or ruched drapes. Each bench would have a card displaying the Kennel Affix. (Actually, in the very early days, Samoyeds could be found on their bench sometimes decked with bows of ribbon.) There were no prizes but it made an impressive display.

Since there were no grooming tables, the next task was to find a wooden table from somewhere on the showground. It was not unknown for a judging table to disappear from a ring in the very early morning! When a dog was ready for its class, it would often be necessary to push through masses of spectators, who would cheerfully applaud each winner. The atmosphere was pleasant and at the end the exhibitors would slowly make their way back home.

There were no classes for Samoyeds at open shows in those days. Betty Cobby, well-known in the Samoyed fraternity, and now a senior citizen, recalls spending the night at a Police Station when she missed her train and had nowhere else to go. Rose Lewis once went to a show at Paignton. The coach stopped off at Bristol. Alas, there they encountered floods and spent the night at Bristol bus depot. They had no food until someone reached them by boat the following morning.

Even when a bitch was taken to be mated, the journey would mostly be undertaken by train and bus. Imagine the disappointment, then, if the mating was not achieved. One fruitless bus journey reduced a well-known exhibitor of the 1950s to tears when the visited stud dog was more interested in digging holes in the garden, almost as if he were suggesting that he would like to bury the visiting bitch!

THE CONTEMPORARY SHOW SCENE

Nowadays so much has changed. In order to reach show venues, many out in the country, a car, usually an estate car or van, is required in order to carry all the dogs and the attendant paraphernalia. These items include a commercial metal grooming table, fold-up or on wheels, a trolley and dog crate. At an open show, this is useful for housing one Sam while another can be groomed on top.

The Kennel Club strictly governs what is permissible on a bench, and this means, literally, ring number, rug and affix. Apart from Crufts, crowds are not usually dense at the ringside and applause is sparse. Today, the training grounds of local sanction shows are just a distant and fond memory. Open Shows are struggling for survival, both through lack of entries and through the dearth of enthusiastic committee members. The majority of exhibitors now appear to want to concentrate on Championships only. In order to try and redress the balance, Breed Clubs are, in some instances, supporting entries at some shows. This means they might offer money, cups, rosettes etc. as inducements for exhibitors to attend, while at the same time, providing names of judges from an approved list.

Numerous new regulations have been brought in by the Kennel Club with regard to the running of shows and all concerned need to be on their toes, since at any time a Kennel Club Field Officer might visit. This Officer will check that all is in order before making a report to the Kennel Club and pointing out any shortcomings to the show management committee. Judges themselves now need to be well-informed on all regulations. They can be fined for any breach, e.g. awarding a dog reserve prize and withholding 3rd, or dismissing a dog from the ring and failing to inform the show secretary.

Other than at Crufts, it is now possible for exhibitors to leave shows early. Hitherto, there was no early removal of exhibits, which meant that a show would retain its atmosphere with many around to witness final awards, rather than the penny numbers found nowadays. I would make an exception as far as Breed Club Championship shows are concerned, since they tend to maintain a happy and cheerful buzz right up to the end. In the 1970s and 80s, there tended to be much more socialisation after showing. It was a regular feature to crowd to the home of any exhibitor living nearest the venue for sustenance and refreshment. Above all, it was just sheer good fun. These days, exhibitors tend to leave early in the day, making a headlong dash to the motorway and home and thereby missing out on the camaraderie shared not so many years ago. The popularity of caravaning at shows now redresses this, but only for a certain few.

A NEW CONCEPT

Initiated in 1995, The Samoyed of the Year has become an annual special event inspired and staged by the Northern Samoyed Society. Best of Breed competitors from each Championship Show are invited to attend and compete

in a knockout competition. This prestigious event is held each November at a hotel in the Nottingham area. Since the competition is combined with a dinner and dance, evening dress is worn. A secret Judge (or Judges) is not announced until the evening of the event. In 1998 a Top Puppy competition was added, using a similar format. Each Best Puppy from a Championship show is similarly invited to participate in a knock-out competition.

BREED RESCUE

Each of the four Samoyed Breed Clubs has a rescue arm. Unpaid volunteers give freely of their own time, undertaking sterling work in order to assist those Samoyeds who, for some reason, need to be re-homed. Funds constantly need to be found in order to support these services, since telephone and kennelling bills can be substantial. In this respect, credit must be given to the Astutus Kennels of Dr and Mrs Hale and Helen Collins who annually stage a rally and exemption show. Proceeds go to the breed rescue service of all four clubs in turn.

The NSS Puppy of the Year 1999: Shianise Bostin Bertie, owned by Mrs Johnston.

The NSS Samoyed of the Year competition 1999. The winner was Ch. Vandreem Imperial Montana, owned by Eileen Cameron and Scott Langlands; runner-up was Ch. Diqust Levi Of Vandreem, owned by Andrea Kirkwood.

14 *THE SAMOYED IN NORTH AMERICA*

Two Samoyeds made an enormous impact in America in the immediate post-war years. In 1946 Dr William Ivens imported Ch. Martingate Snowland Taz from England at the age of two years. His influence on the breed was phenomenal. He sired 28 Champions, accruing 54 BOBs and numerous Group placings. In 1954 and 1955 he also was the winner of the Wimunstrev Stud dog trophy, which is no longer offered.

In 1949, Bernice Ashdown of the Wychwood Kennel imported Eng. Ch. Princess Silvertips Of Kobe. She was a much admired bitch, who had collected nine CCs in England. She quickly became an American Champion and was mated with Ch. Martingate Snowland Taz. The result was an outstanding litter which produced five Champions and two BIS Winners. She went on to have an amazing show career with 48 BOBs and two BIS in 1951 and 1953. All this and four litters as well – what a bitch! Her son Ch. Silver Spray At Wychwood went Best Samoyed at the Westminster Show for four years consecutively, just like his dad.

THE RISE IN POPULARITY

In 1956, Bernice Ashdown imported yet another sensational dog, Eng. Ch. Americ Of Kobe. At his very first show he was made Best in Show. He went on to become an American Champion and consistent Group Winner, remaining unbeaten in breed classes. It is acknowledged that this illustrious kennel made a wonderful contribution to the Samoyed breed in America with the perpetuation of sound-quality stock. There was a period in the 1950s when a Wychwood Samoyed went BIS every year. This record is to be truly admired.

With all these wonderful winning dogs, no wonder Samoyeds gained in popularity. They were also taking part in a number of different activities – obedience and sled racing. An important dog of the 1950s was Ch. Yurok Of Whitecliff, known as Rocky. He was jointly owned by Percy and Lena Matherson and Jean Blank. He was to accrue 136 BOBs, 98 Group Placings and a BIS All Breeds.

Other important Kennels of this era were Top Acres, Silver Moon, Encino, Sam O'Khan and Karasea. Ch. Nordly's

Am. Can. Bah. Ch. Polar Mist Dr Pepper.

Sammy, owned by the Doyles, had a string of wins in the late 1950s and was a grandson of Ch. Martingate Snowland Taz.

1964 saw the introduction of a separate Specialty show for the Samoyed Club of America. Hitherto, the Specialty had been held in conjunction with an All Breeds Show.

SILVERACRES
Harold and Doris McLaughlin of the Silveracres Kennel obtained their first Samoyed in 1954 when she was found abandoned and chasing sheep. One of their later dogs, Ch. Nachalnik Of Drayalene, known as Chief, became the top stud dog in the US for 10 years between 1973 to 1983. He was to sire 45 Champions which included both Canadian and Mexican Champions.

ALADDIN, ORION AND POLAR MIST
Joyce and Joseph Johnson started the Aladdin Kennel. Later they were to produce Am. Ch. Aladdin's Dominator, called Note, who was much admired. In 1965 Sharon Hurst appeared on the scene with the Orion Kennel. She was to own a number of really good Samoyeds and, much later, obtained Ch. Sansaska's Omarson Of Orion, known as Omi, who was to be a BIS Winner in 1986. Sharon eventually purchased, from Lynette Hanson, Am. Can. Mex. Int. Ch. Orion's Bud Light Of Polar Mist who, in 1991, was Top Winning Samoyed and Top Stud dog. Sharon was a top breeder in 1989 and also in 1993. Bud Light was a top producing dog also in 1993, siring 20 Champions.

1965 also saw the emergence of a kennel which was to become famous worldwide. Lynette Hanson of Polar Mist Samoyeds started, during this year, with a pet Samoyed. Her foundations were to be Ch. McKenzie's Polar Mist Nikki and Polar Mist Baerstone Nishka. She went on to breed, own or co-own over 100 Champions. Am. Can. Ch. Polar Mist Ain't She Foxy was a Top Brood Bitch in 1984. The most famous dog, however, to emerge from this kennel was Am. Can. Bahamian Ch. Polar Mist Dr Pepper, by Ch. Beleya Sergeant Pepper ex Am. Can. Ch. Pepsi Kola Of Polar Mist (see Chapter Eight: Record Breakers), who was the top winning owner-handled Samoyed in history. Lynette co-owned Pepper with John Ronald and his wife and he lived with them. Pepper has a record 13 BIS, 144 Group Placements and seven Specialty BIS. Lynette Hanson remarried and became Lynette Hanson-Blue. She also found time for Obedience work.

NORTHSTARR, WINTERFROST AND KIPPERIC
The Northstarr Kennels of Robert and Patricia Hritzo have yet another admirable record. They were to become

well known as the breeder-owners of Am. Can. Ch. North Starr's King's Ransom. As a puppy he was handled by their ten-year-old daughter, who herself went on to win a Top Junior Handlers award at Westminster. He won eleven All Breed BIS and was the first Samoyed in more than twenty years to be in the Top Ten Working Dogs in the States. He was sire to over 30 Champions including Ch. North Starr's Bosun, who became the Top Winning dog in Columbia. Altogether, they have bred or owned 48 Champions.

In 1967, Louise O'Connell started her Winterfrost Kennels, basically breeding with Kondako lines. She was living in Canada until 1991, then moved to Pennsylvania. She focused on soundness, laid-back temperament, balanced effortless movement, breed type and style. In 1989, Louise bred Ch. Winterfrost Gyrfalcon, known as Gyr, who features in the Record Breakers section (Chapter Eight). Tragically, the best bitch and the second best dog of Gyr's litter were killed in an airline tragedy and, as a result, Louise no longer flies her dogs to shows.

The Kipperic Kennel of Don and Dot Hodges was also started in the mid-60s when their first Samoyed was purchased for obedience work. The Kipperic Kennel has an impressive breeding record and has owned around 60 Champions. Am. Can. Ch. Kipperic Kandu Of Suruka Orr CD was a top winning Samoyed in the US in 1974. Ch. Kipperic Heritage Heroine was Top Winning Bitch in 1989. Other major winners from this Kennel include Ch. Kipperic Sparkson, Ch. Kipperic Flashback and Ch. Kipperic Sunny Peterson.

INDEPENDENT CLUBS

By 1969, there was a new structure to the Samoyed Club of America. Although this remained the parent Club, local clubs were allowed to become independent. Robert 'Bob' Ward became the President. Also in 1969, Ch. Sayan Of Woodland equalled Ch. Nordly's Sammy's record of four Specialty wins. Seventeen Champions were produced by this partnership over a fourteen-year period, with Ch. Kondako's Dancing Bear featuring strongly.

THE GROWTH OF DUAL-PURPOSE DOGS

The Bubbling Oakes Kennel of Jack and Amelia Price began in the early seventies. They were to be involved in many facets of the Samoyed as a breed – Obedience, conformation, sledding, weight-pulling. One of their bitches was a cracker and became very famous. She had the delightful name of Am. Can. Ch. Bubbles La Rue Of Oakwood. I remember seeing her photograph on a Samoyed calendar of that time. She was the SCA Top Bitch 1975-1976. She was the All-time top-winning bitch in breed history for a long time.

The Grey Ghost Kennel of Wayne and Janet Heffington started in 1970. They made up 27 Champions and also had an All Champion Sled Team which is used for local events. Mardee Ward-Fanning's Hoof N'Paw Kennels were also started in 1970. She was to take over where her parents Bob and Dolly Ward left off, using imports from Denmark alongside English bloodlines. Mardee owns dual-purpose dogs, working and show. They take part in conformation, sledding, obedience, therapy, agility and weight-pulling. She has had mega success and is currently right at the top. Her foundation sire was Am. Mex. Ch. The Hoof N'Paw White Knight (more in the 1990s section). In 1971, Phoebe Faulmann formed the Heritage Kennel; 30 Champions were produced including a Mexican BIS Winner.

SOME TOP WINNERS

A lot happened in 1972. Danny and Chris Middleton purchased their first Samoyed and were interested in obedience. They went on to get involved with breeding and showing and become famous with a dog who was to be the top winning Samoyed in the history of the Breed. He was Am. Ch. Quicksilver's Razz Ma Tazz. His wins are mindblowing and Tazz appears in the Record Breakers section (Chapter Eight). He was born in 1981 and was to produce a son, Ch. Kolinica Quicksilver Jazzman, who, among other awards, was to become a multiple Group Winner.

In that year, Derek and Marilyn Gitelson started their Sansaska Kennel; Marilyn also became the Secretary of the Samoyed Club of America. From the beginning they had great success, starting with Ch. Noresemar O'Khan's Milka, and had numerous Champions, one of which was Ch. Sansaska's Omarsun Of Orion BIS BISS and a Top Ten Samoyed. Also in 1972, Bob and Dolly Ward bought from Gerald and Kath Mitchell in England a dog they considered to be almost a double of their own Ch. Starchak. This was Kiskas Karaholme Cherokee, known as Painter, bred by Tom and Joyce Stamp. He was also of similar breeding through his sire and dam (Ch. Cavalier Of Crensa ex Lisa Of Crownie). He was quickly made an American Champion and became SCA Top Stud Dog in 1980.

Am. Ch. Quicksilver's Razz Ma Tazz.

In 1975 the Danica Kennel got under way with breeding lines from Sam O'Khan, Kondako and Silver Moon. Westwind Samoyeds owned by Timothy Malueg commenced in 1976 when Can. Bermudian Ch. Karlot's Jak Frost Of Westwind was born. He was to sire two All Champion litters and sired some of the top winning stock in both Canada and America. Tragically he died of bloat.

The Kiriskella Samoyeds of Geoff and Brenda Abbott started in 1978. In 1984, Geoff drove a sled team which became the first team to win the SCA award for Top Sled Team. The Seelah Kennels produced Am. Ch. Di Murdock Of Seelah, SCA Top Winning Samoyed in 1979 and 1980 and Top Stud dog in 1982.

MOONLIGHT AND FROSTYACRES

One of the most illustrious kennels of the last twenty years is the Moonlighter Kennel of Wayne and Jeanne Nonhof. Their foundation bitch was Moonlighter's Altai Star Mist and their record is second to none. Champions produced are just too numerous to mention, their most famous dog being Am. Ch. Moonlighter's Ima Bark Star TT. This incredible dog sired no less than sixty Champions. For a time Jeanne Nonhof was President of the SCA.

During the 1980s the Hoof N'Paw Kennels continued with outstanding success in all fields. Among their many worthy Champions of this time were Am. Ch. Hoof N'Paws In The Buff, Am. Can. Ch. Hoof N'Paws Knight Rider and Am. Ch. Hoof N'Paws Ramblin' Rose.

Karlin McFarlane's Frostyacres Kennels came into existence when she purchased Ch. Karalot's Hotshot Of Windsong. He went into the Top Ten list of Sires in 1982, and in the same year Ch. Frostyacres I've Been Samkist was Top Brood Bitch. A later bitch, Ch. Frostyacres Born Blonde was BISS in 1996 and a multiple Group winner. From Amelia and Jack Feinberg came Am. Ch. Northwind's Black Magic and Ch. Northwind Running Bear. Bear was The No.1 Samoyed in America in 1981. Undoubtedly, however, their best well-known Samoyed, co-owned with Esther and Robert Halmi, was Multi Ch. Northwind's Rising Star. Star features in Record Breakers (Chapter Eight).

Another winning dog of this time was Sandra Duke's Ch. Image's The Barrister. He sired several Champions. No.1 Samoyed bitch in 1989 was Ch. Sitkin's Simply Scrumptious.

MORE CONTEMPORARY WINNERS
The Saratoga Samoyeds of Heidi and Don Nieman started in 1987. In 1994 and 1995 Ch. Saratoga's Speed Of Sound, known as Mach, was the Top Producing Stud Dog and a multiple Group Winner.

Am. Ch. Sanorka's Moonlight Gambler.

Previous to that, the No.1 Samoyed in 1992 and 1993 was Cheryl Wagner's Am. Bermudian Ch. Tarahills Everybody Duck. He had 14 BIS wins and produced 35 Champions.

Am. Mex. Int. Ch. Sunburst's Torch Of Liberty became one of the five best Samoyeds in the USA. He became a Top Producing Stud dog in 1992 and 1993. Campaigned by Jimmy Moses, Ch. Ren J's Go Go Dancer BIS BISS was the SCA Top Winning Bitch 1993 and 1994, also owned by Janice Hovelmann.

1994 and 1995 saw Ch. Tega Joe Knows TT, owned and bred by Terry and Gail Campbell, become No.1 Samoyed. He was also a Top Ten Working Dog in 1994 and a Top Twenty Working Dog in 1995. He amassed 184 BOBs, five BISS and 120 Group Placings.

Janice Hovelmann's marvellous Am. Ch. Sanorka Moonlight Gambler was SCA Top Stud Dog in 1991, 1994, 1995 and 1996. He has produced over thirty Champions. Ch. Wolf River's Terra must be mentioned. Owned and bred by Kay Hallberg, she was known as an outstanding bitch, featuring in the Top Five Samoyeds in the USA. She pursued a dual-purpose race sledding career, which possibly curtailed her showing activities.

Bred by John and Kathy Regan, Am. Can. Int. Ch. Li'l Paws Sun Of Torch BIS, CGX, owned by Diane Dobson of Galaxy Samoyeds, became a Multiple BIS Winner and one of Canada's Top Five Samoyeds for 1997. SCA Top Dog for 1997 and Samoyed Club of Canada's Top Dog for 1998 was Ch. Sanorka's Moonlight Trip T'Rex J.

SCA Top Bitch for 1998 was Ch. Hoof N'Paw's A Rose Is A Rose, who is fast becoming a legend and features in Record Breakers, Chapter Eight. The Hoof N'Paw's Kennels of Mardee Ward-Fanning must be one of the major contemporary influences in the USA. Meanwhile Ch. Hoof N'Paws Midknight Maxx WDX, CGC, TDI also became a Top Samoyed in 1998.

THE POINTS SYSTEM
In the USA points towards major awards are compiled by different organisations in different ways. These organisations include: Samoyed Club of America (SCA), Samoyed Quarterly, Dogs in Canada Points systems, Dogs in Canada Magazine, Canine Chronicle, Phillips and Eukannba.

ABBREVIATIONS
Names of dogs in North America are frequently shown with initials after their name. Below is an explanation of those abbreviations.

AM	–	Award of Merit
AX	–	Agility Excellent
BB	–	Best of Breed
BISS	–	Best in Specialty Show
CD	–	Companion Dog
CDX	–	Companion Dog Excellent
CGX	–	Canine Good Citizen
CH	–	Champion
CT	–	Champion Tracker
HC	–	Herding Champion
HIC	–	Herding Instinct Certified
HI	–	Herding Intermediate
HS	–	Herding Started
HT	–	Herding Tested
HX	–	Herding Excellent
MX	–	Master Agility
NA	–	Novice Agility
OA	–	Open Agility
OTCH	–	Obedience Trial Champion
TD	–	Tracking Dog
TDX	–	Tracking Dog Excellent
TT	–	Temperament Tested
TDI	–	Therapy Dog International
UD	–	Utility Dog
UDT	–	Utility Dog Tracking
VST	–	Variable Surface Tracker

There is no doubt that in the USA Samoyed fanciers work their Samoyeds very much more than in the UK. This must make life so much more interesting both for the Sams and for their owners. In the UK the only title to be added after a name, besides Champion, is JW – Junior Warrant.

I would like to pay tribute to Dolly Ward, who died in 1998. I was lucky enough to meet her a few years ago. She gave so much to the Samoyed breed and her expertise was second to none. She is sadly missed by the worldwide Samoyed fraternity.

THE SAMMY ANGELS

The Sammy Angels are a fundraising group for Samoyed Rescue. The group was founded by Rosemary Babb in October 1997, in honour of Toby, a rescue Samoyed who was killed by his new owner. Many Samoyed lovers were devastated by Toby's death. Rosemary founded the Sammy Angels to ensure that some good would come of this sad incident, that Toby would not be forgotten, and that other Samoyeds in need would receive help. When Rosemary told her husband David that she needed a name for the new fundraiser, he immediately suggested "The Sammy Angels".

Before announcing the fundraiser, Rosemary contacted two Samoyed owners, Catherine Rainwater of the US and breeder Marjorie Hueston of Canada, to ask for their opinions. Both wanted to sign up. Each Sammy Angel pledges $100 a year to help with medical and other expenses for rescued Samoyeds. Some Angels also make pledges in others' names, so they can also be part of the group.

Many of the pledges are in honour of, or in memory of, a beloved dog or person. In May 1999 there were 126 Sammy Angels from the United States and Canada, which meant $12,600 a year pledged for special needs rescue dogs. Angels' interests include conformation and breeding, obedience, therapy dogs, rescue, sledding, and "just pets".

The Angels work through established Samoyed Rescue groups. Groups in the US and Canada are eligible. When a rescue group needs help, they contact Rosemary. She collects all the necessary information and forwards it to the other Sammy Angels. Each Angel decides if they want to help with that particular case, and if so, how much they would like to donate. All decisions are made by the individual donors, and all funds go directly to the rescue groups.

By May 1999 almost $11,000 had been paid out to benefit 54 dogs. Handling donations in this way avoids the need for people to donate money in advance that might sit in a bank for months. It avoids the need for setting limits on the money available per dog, for a committee to make decisions (and maybe fight about them), and for reinventing the wheel every time a case comes up.

It is an easy, fast way to connect those who need help with those who are willing and able to give it. And it leaves all decisions in the hands of the individual donors. Most Angels are online, and most communication is by e-mail. Those who are not online can also be part of the group by sending their donation in advance. Donations are usually used in the next case that comes up. These Angels are notified by phone or letter before their donation is sent to a rescue group and they receive full details of the case. The following are some of the dogs the Sammy Angels have helped.

Cotton Cotton was nine years old when her owners decided they did not want her any more. They gave her to Northern Illinois Samoyed Assistance after they failed to sell her. They could not recall when she had last received any medical care. She was seriously ill, with

145

heartworm and mammary tumors, and needed to be spayed. The Sammy Angels helped pay for her medical care. It was nine months before Cotton was well enough to be adopted by her new owner, who was waiting for her. By the time she was ready to go home, she was so popular that NISA had a going-away party for her.

Cody, Belle and Nya Cody and Belle are former show dogs, and Nya is Belle's daughter. Their owner committed suicide after battling alcoholism and drug abuse for several years, leaving her Samoyeds tied to trees in her neighbour's orchard. They had been badly neglected. They had whipworm, and toenails so long they curled into their feet, so they had trouble walking. Nya was completely unsocialized, had never been in a house, and had to learn to live life without her mother. Cody was very underweight, had foxtails in his feet, and had to be completely shaved due to mats and foxtails. Cody, Belle, and Nya were rescued by San Francisco Samoyed Rescue. The Sammy Angels paid for Nya and Belle to be boarded with and treated by a professional behaviorist for a month so they would be adoptable. All three found new homes.

Calypso, Sam and Metika This trio was rescued from a puppy mill in North Carolina. Calypso and Sam had been injured in a fight with other dogs. Calypso was badly injured, including head, leg and chest wounds, and an 8" long laceration on her skull, and was in shock. She had had puppies about nine weeks previously. Only three of her eight puppies had survived. One of those had already been sold, and the two remaining puppies were killed in the dog fight.

Calypso was injured trying to defend her puppies from the other dogs. Sam's foot was injured in the dog fight. Metika, who may be Calypso's daughter, was in the best shape of the three. All were badly matted, malnourished, and had mange. The Sammy Angels paid for Calypso, Sam, and Metika's medical care. All three were adopted. Calypso was adopted by one of the Sammy Angels who helped in her case.

Kodi Kodiak, age five, had severe hip dysplasia. He was left in a shelter, and was picked up by the Central Arizona Samoyed Club. It was love at first sight for his rescuers. In spite of his pain and a bad limp, when he came out of the cage at the shelter his tail was wagging. The Sammy Angels helped pay for a hip replacement for Kodi, and he was adopted by his foster home.

Rosemary would like to extend the Angels programme for Samoyeds in other countries. She can be contacted via: PO Box 675, Brighton, CO 80601 USA; EMail: Samy Angels @ aol.com; Web page: http://members.aol.com/alorah/samang. html

CANADA
The earliest Samoyeds were thought to have been brought into Canada in the early 1900s by Leonhard Seppala, a Norwegian sled dog owner. In 1913, the very first Samoyed was exhibited in the city of Victoria, British Columbia, but it was 1925 before Samoyeds were registered by the Canadian Kennel Club. At that time, four Samoyeds were registered, having been imported from the United States, but with their pedigrees showing ancestors from the UK.

During the Second World War,

George Davies of the Kindon Kennel in Ontario was instrumental in helping the breed to remain in existence in Canada. 1940 saw Ch. Spark Of Altai become the first Samoyed to go Best in Show in Canada. Numerically, the breed continued to increase and by 1957 the Canadian Samoyed Club, Inc. was formed. By 1959 a Breed Standard was introduced. In 1966, the Samoyed Association of Canada was founded and this is, today, the only current National Samoyed Club in Canada. The Club also recognises obedience awards.

Samoyed fanciers in Canada participate in a number of events with their dogs, including Agility, Pack-Hiking, Therapy, Flyball and Weight Pulling. There are local breed clubs. One of them, the Edmonton Samoyed Club, organises an overnight camp-out every July with all these doggy events and a fun match.

In 1993, a new Breed Standard was approved. This brought the Standard more in line with the AKC, as the height was agreed as the same and more specific detail was included. There have been a number of breeders in Canada who have actively contributed to maintaining the quality of the breed. Twenty years ago, I was lucky to meet Pat Stoneham of the Khingham Kennels and be invited to her home to meet her dogs. She was kindness itself and had some lovely Sams.

For many years, Dr Bob Gaskin, a veterinarian, was the Secretary of The Canadian Samoyed Club. He is the owner of the famous Chaena, a Ch. Kiskas Karaholme Cherokee grandson, tracing back to the very best of English stock. There follows information from some well-respected kennels in Canada today.

SHEBASKA

Frank and Helga Gruber of Cheltenham, Ontario, kennel name Shebaska, bought their first puppy in 1968. After meeting Pat and Bill Stoneham at a show, they acquired from them Khingham's Queen Of Sheba CD who was to become their foundation bitch. She was out of the successful English Snowland, Snowcryst and Crownie lines. In their first litter, the Grubers had two Champions. The Grubers continued to use this successful breeding programme. Some of the dogs of which they are most proud are Ch. Khingham's Chu The Magnificent and litter mates Can. Am. Ch. Shebaska's Diamond Dazzler and his litter sister Ch. Shebaski's Vashti Bathsheba. Also out of a bitch with a strong Kobe background came the exquisite Can. Am. Ch. Shebaska's Cashmere, Helga's constant companion at fourteen years of age.

POLOBAR

Barbara Heal of Polobar Samoyed purchased her first Samoyed in 1969. She later acquired a female puppy, Chakka's Siberian Soul Sister, whom she used as her foundation bitch. Barbara very much admired the English Samoyeds and accordingly bred this bitch to the English import, Can. Am. Eng. Ch. Fairvilla Istvan Of Airebis. Four out of the resulting five puppies became Champions. In 1973, with Can. Ch. Polobar's Prince Albert, she was delighted to receive, from the late Cathy Sutton from England, a Best Canadian Bred Award. Later on she combined her best English/Canadian lines with the best of the US, through Ch. Moonlighter's Luna Bark Star. This resulted in one of the prettiest bitches ever bred by Barbara; she was to become Can. Ch.

147

Can. Ch. Polobar's Prince Albert sired by Can. Am. UK Ch. Fairvilla Istvan Of Airebis.

Can. Ch. Vanderbilt's Pink Parachutes.

Polobar's Bad News Bear, and from her came many other Champions.

VANDERBILT

Judi Elford is the current President of the Canadian Samoyed Club. She and her husband Blair began their love affair with Samoyeds as teenagers in 1977 in Newfoundland. Two Samoyeds acquired at that time were from English Snowland and Kobe stock. They were Ch. Shebaska's Ebonys Opposite CDX, a male, and a bitch Ch. Wenette's Morning Frost CD. Enormous success followed on with Multi-BIS Can. Am. Ch. Vanderbilt's Secretariat and Can. Am. Ch. Vanderbilt Neon Nightingale ROMC. Over the years, further quality lines were introduced. From Am. Ch. Iceway's Ice Breaker came BIS Ch. Polarmist Break The Bank and then Ch. Mystical Marla Of Vanderbilt. From legendary Am. BIS BISS Ch. Wolf River's Terra came Can. Ch. Wolf River's

High As A Kite ROM and, later, Ch. Wolf River's Vanderbilt Mesa. Further dogs from this kennel appear in Chapter Eight: Record Breakers. The Kennel's aim has always been to produce healthy, mellow-tempered, unexaggerated and totally sound-moving Samoyeds of glorious type, capable of doing the jobs so ably performed by their ancestors. Judi's ambition is to see the reality of an International Symposium on the Samoyed, bringing fanciers and experts together from round the globe to discuss the breed and its future. An exciting prospect.

SNOWGHOST

The Snowghost Kennel of Mike and Lee Palutke was established in 1980. Their first bitch's pedigree included some impressive Canadian dogs based on English Kobe imports and a male from top US lines. They have had enormous success and were Canadian Top Breeders in 1990, 1991 and 1995. BIS Ch. Snowghosts Here There Be Tygers became No.1 Samoyed in Canada in 1997, while still a puppy, a feat achieved by only one other Samoyed in breed history. In 1998, Ch. Snowghosts Hot July Moon attained Championship Status as a Junior puppy. In both the USA and Canada, Snowghost Samoyeds have gained recognition in conformation and Obedience and are involved in sledding, both recreational and racing.

TAKENAK
Dr Leslie Jocelyn and Dr Lawrence Homik share the Takenak Kennel name. Although Leslie's parents had a rescue Samoyed in 1970, they first became seriously involved in Samoyeds in 1985. From a first breeding was kept BIS and BISS Am. Ch. Takenak's May King Mischief, who was No.1 Samoyed in 1989. Multiple BIS and BISS Am. Ch. Takenak's Make My Day, known as Cally, has a Canadian BIS and four BISS. Shown by Lawrence Homik, this dog was the father of yet another outstanding female from this Kennel, Can. Ch. Takenak's What's Up Doc, known as Bugsy. At seven months, she gained her Canadian Championship with many Best Puppy awards and Group placements. She was No.1 Bitch, No.1 Owner Handled and No.2 Samoyed in Canada in 1996. Both these two have now received their WSX titles from the

Can. Ch. Takenak's What's Up Doc.

Samoyed Club of America. This is for participating in excursion sledding and it stands for Working Samoyed Excellent. NOTE: Although a Herding Group was added to the Groups in Canada in the 1980s, the Samoyed continues to be shown in the Working Group. ROM means Register of Merit. In Canada the names of dogs who sire more than ten Champions are placed on this register.

15

THE SAMOYED WORLDWIDE

AUSTRALIA
By Marjorie Steele and Helen Gabb

Australia has had a much longer association with Samoyeds than most people realise. Dogs that were no longer useful on the Antarctic expeditions of the time were off-loaded in Sydney, New South Wales in the early 1900s. Ernest Kilburn-Scott stumbled upon Antarctic Buck who was an exhibit at the Sydney Zoo. When Kilburn-Scott returned to England, Antarctic Buck went too. During the early days of Antarctic exploration a number of Samoyeds found their way to the seaport of Sydney. Few had their lives documented. However, another expedition Samoyed, Ambrose, was given in 1909 to Professor Edgeworth David, the geologist on the Shackleton Expedition. Ambrose quickly became a family favourite. His photograph has survived and is printed in the book *Passages of Time*. Sadly, Ambrose died of distemper soon after his return from Antarctic. Records do not remain of other Samoyeds known to have landed here. Records are available of a Samoyed sled team being used by the New South Wales Tourist Bureau at Charlotte's Pass in the Australian Snowy Mountains. The team was kennelled at The Chalet and in summer months went out about three times a week on runs to keep them fit for their winter work. The team once pulled out an Air Force plane, salvaged after crashing on Carruthers Peak.

EARLY IMPORTS
The Samoyed Club of Victoria has shown great initiative and has now produced two pedigree books *Samoyed Champions of Australia*. The first volume relates to dogs born prior to 1976. Volume 2 relates to dogs born and imported from 1976 to 1992. Ron and Lorraine Addison have been instrumental in working on this project.

Aus. Ch. Yukon Queen born 1929 (UK Imp.) was imported by Mr J. Maike of Sydney, who, together with Miss L. Irving of Victoria, was an early breeder of Samoyeds. He also imported Aus. Ch. Snow White (Imp.) from the UK and later White Ripple Of Kobe (Imp. UK), born in 1938. He also bred the first recorded Australian Samoyed Champion,

A group of Samoyeds in the Australian bush.

Aus. Ch. Blackeyed Susan, from Yukon Queen and Snow White. Apart from Mr Maike, some of the earlier people to import Samoyeds from the UK were Miss E. Bradshaw, Mr M. Enkhart, Len and Joan Rowse of Zahmah Kennels; and, in 1954, Yvonne Sydenham-Clarke of Kalina Kennels imported her foundation bitch, Icemist Beauty Of Kobe (Imp. UK). Joan Rowse's dedication in keeping early records has greatly assisted in documenting the breed in Australia. Much of the stock imported over the years by Kalina Kennels still shows up in today's pedigrees more than 45 years on.

EARLY EXHIBITORS
The Eleban Kennels of George and Merle Jacques acquired their first Samoyed, Aus. Ch. Petchoria Snow Chief, in 1953 from George's cousin. At Snow Chief's second show he went on to win Best Exhibit in Show All Breeds (the first New South Wales Samoyed to achieve this award). Eleban went on to become a significant force in the development of New South Wales Samoyeds: they later brought in the benefits of new bloodlines through using the Victorian Kalina imports at stud over their bitches and also brought in Kalina pups who matured to be winning breeding and exhibition stock. A number of these Samoyeds won various challenges at the Sydney, Brisbane and Melbourne Royal shows. The last Eleban Samoyed Champion produced was born in late 1974. He was Aust. Ch. Eleban Yuki Baronoff owned by Moonsnow Kennels (Stan and Lena Smith) who were successful exhibitors and breeders of Samoyeds for 30 years.

The Bellinden Kennels of Joyce Jones imported in the early 1960s Aust. Ch. Pride of Kildare (Imp. Ireland) and several more later. Bellinden produced a number of Champions. During the same period the Sleighland Kennels of Mr and Mrs C. Randall were successful breeders and exhibitors, breeding numbers of Champions, mostly based on Kalina stock.

The Suomi Kennels of Mr and Mrs Ron Impey brought in the benefit of a number of Victorian-bred Samoyeds who left their mark on the breed at that time – the late 1950s to mid-1960s. Probably the most famous of these were Aust. Ch. Wyndalon Silver Czar (the most successful conformation ring Australian-bred Samoyed of his time) and Aust. Ch. Kalina Kobeisky, winner of the New South Wales Samoyed Club's Sires Sweepstakes 1961-62, 1963-64, 1964-65, and 1967-68. Suomi also brought to New South Wales a number of lovely bitches; probably the most of important of these was Aust. Ch. Lynstar Tambina.

The Taz Kennels of Bob and Clara Willis obtained in 1962 a daughter of Aust. Ch. Suomi Myth and Aust. Ch.

Eureka of Kobe (Imp. UK), who became Aust. Ch. Suvarka Tanya. Tanya was mated to Aust. Ch. Starya of Kobe (Imp. UK) and Eng. Ch. Darryl of Tamitsa (Imp. UK) and Aust. Ch. Kalina Silver Blaze. Each of these matings produced Champions. Taz, together with the Rotoiti Kennels of Dennis and Pat Hosking, imported the only Samoyed dog to come to Australia from Canada, Canadian Ch. Kristik's Satin Silhouette (Imp. Can). Taz is now New South Wales' oldest Samoyed breeding and exhibiting kennel. They have bred numerous BIS and Challenge winners.

The small Sever Kennels of Stephen and Helen Gabb started in 1965. Matings for many years were based upon the lines of Kalina's import, Aust. Eng. Ch. Imperial Rebel of Kobe (Imp. UK). Aust. Ch. Sever Imperator CD, born in 1970, holds the New South Wales Samoyed Club's Dog Point Score record, winning for five consecutive years (1972-1977). He won the Sydney Royal Challenge at 9 years and 9 months of age. Of the early exhibitors in Victoria, Mr and Mrs Young's Kalina and Alpayo are still active in the show ring.

MAKING AN AUSTRALIAN CHAMPION

In every state of Australia – West Australia, South Australia, New South Wales, Victoria, Australian Capital Territory, Queensland and the Northern Territory – All-Breed Dog Shows are held both days of every weekend. The shows take the form of either an Open Show or a Championship Show. It is at the Championship shows that a dog or bitch earns points to make it up to an Australian Champion. One hundred points must be accumulated, with dogs and bitches earning one point, plus one point for each animal of the same sex and breed exhibited in every class except Baby Puppy. A further 25 points are granted on winning the group. A good dog can earn its title in just four Championship Shows. A good dog who continues to be shown and constantly wins Challenge points will be granted the title of Australian Grand Champion once he or she accumulates 1,000 points. The title of Australian Grand Champion was introduced at the beginning of 1998. This title has already been won by a handful of Samoyeds in Australia.

Of the six states, only West Australia and Northern Territory do not have Samoyed Clubs. Although the state clubs run autonomously, they are encouraged to be members of the National Samoyed Council which was formed in 1988. The Council is directly reportable to the ANKC on matters relating to the Samoyed, but is only able to make decisions on the breed as voted on by the member states. The Samoyed Club of Victoria is the oldest of the Samoyed Clubs in Australia, holding its 50th Anniversary Show in 1994. The state clubs hold regular meetings, publish newsletters, run their own shows each year, and have rescue services. It is not unusual around Christmas time to see Santa being pulled in a sled by a team of Samoyeds.

The Dog World in Australia is governed by the Australian National Kennel Control (ANKC), and each state is represented and governed by their own council which must report directly to the ANKC. The current Breed Standard is the same as the English Standard.

DOG SHOWS

Because Australia is such a large country,

152

the distances between major cities can be a full day's travel, so exhibitors from other states do not normally travel the distance unless it is an important show. The various state clubs welcome interstate exhibitors to their Open shows and Championship shows. Once every three years a National Championship Show is held and the host club rotates, as does the venue. The first-ever National was held in Melbourne, Victoria in 1988 and was won by Aus. Ch. Kalina Uki Tochka, the judge being Mr Robin Newhouse of the UK. The most recent National was held in Australian Capital Territory in May 1998 and judged by Mrs Beryl Grounds and won by Aus. Ch. Zamora Kryshar Katarina. The major All Breed Agricultural Show is in Melbourne and attracts an entry of around 6,000 dogs, including about 100 Samoyeds. In 1995, Aus. Ch. Aldonza Kistas Kid, owned and handled by Fay Tucker, won the Group.

Sydney Royal Easter Show is a slightly smaller show but equally important. These shows are usually judged by International Judges. Samoyeds have had major wins over the years. In 1960, Ch. Starya Of Kobe, owned by Yvonne Sydenham-Clarke, went BIS. In 1971, BIS was won by Marilyn Roulston's Aus. Ch. Lourdale Tzarmak. In 1989 Tucker and Steele's Aus. Ch. Aldonza Suki Surprise won the group. In 1994, Fay Tucker's Ch. Aldonza Kiss And Tell went BIS. In 1996 Aus. Ch. Tobalsk Royal Secret, handled by Julie Oates and bred by Leonie Waymoult, went BIS, and in 1998 Ch. Aldonza Kistas Kid won the Group. A marvellous achievement for the breed as a whole.

DOG BREEDERS

Because of the vast distances separating the main cities where the larger shows are held and the greater number of exhibitors are to be found, matings between dogs from different states do not occur as frequently as one would imagine. A lot of planning and some good timing is involved if one wishes to use a stud residing in a different part of the country. Driving from Melbourne to Sydney takes 10 hours. A flight is a bit over one hour but, as the airports are always on the outskirts of the cities, depending on where the breeder lives it could be a round trip of three hours just to get to the airport to drop off or pick up a bitch being sent for mating. Obviously, unless the animal is sent well before the actual deed is to be done, this can be quite stressful for the bitch and can sometimes be a waste of time!

Most suburban homes in Australia are limited to two or three dogs by local council regulations, so serious breeders are forced to move to rural or semi-rural areas to enable them to run several dogs. Some people have to move out of the city quite a fair distance, as land within, say, 100 kms of the city centre is quite expensive. Living near the country centres is a lot more affordable, but jobs have to be considered. Another factor is the distance the exhibitor then has to travel to the more important shows. So, many problems face those people who have, over a time, become dedicated to their breed and wish to introduce long-term breeding programmes.

THE LOOK OF THE AUSTRALIAN SAMOYED

Some time back the look of Samoyeds in the show ring was changing. Creeping

Aust. Ch. Alanza Regmar Rebel.

in were poor movers, snipy heads and long weepy coats, and judges' eyes were becoming used to seeing this type of Samoyed. Some Samoyed exhibitors started communicating with other breeders, gaining a better understanding of not only the good points but the faults of their own dogs. It was recognised that to improve the breed, people had to find a way of correcting their "kennel blindness". They became resolved to change this picture to a better interpretation of the Breed Standard.

Eventually a more athletic Samoyed started to show up in the ring, one that had a neck, was not too heavily boned, with correct stand-off coat, a better balanced head, smaller well-furred ears – a dog that could move. This was a dog that could run all day with a herd of reindeer, be nimble enough to guide them out of trouble, able to jump ice crevassses if necessary and a coat that

would not be weighed down by ice and snow. Several breeders, buoyed on by this better-looking and performing Samoyed started to put into place positive breeding programmes, for this was a Samoyed that was appreciated by overseas and more experienced local judges. Most of the top breeders are now very particular about the fitness of their dogs, keeping them well exercised, well-muscled, lean and correctly fed to encourage good coat and soundness of body and mind. One dog in particular of the "new look" that comes to mind is Aus. Ch. Alanza Regmar Rebel. His movement and conformation were probably among the best seen in a Samoyed in this country.

BREEDERS AND EXHIBITORS
Victoria has the best depth of quality in Samoyeds and has had for some time. Many of the kennels have been established for several years and have played an important part in the development of the breed, producing Champion stock – Alpayo, Alveka, Amir, Amundsen, Bloric, Eskimane, Kalaska, Kirani, Lauranook, Leonieglen, Mezen, Monaltyo, Polastar, Silvasam, Snerzok, Snowbrook, Vyatka.

One of the more successful kennels in Victoria, Elgianto, owned by Oates and Phillips and registered in 1964, bred a dog, Grand Ch. Elgianto Heza Star, who showed with great success for several years. His progeny have gone on to emulate his prowess. Novaskaya Royal Blaze (Imp. UK) has sired several top winning Samoyeds; not the least is the winner of the 1996 Sydney Royal Easter Show, Aus. Ch. Tobalsk Royal Secret. His sons have already had great success in the ring.

Zamora Kennels, owned by Glenda Hustwaite, started with Kalina stock. Zamora's breeding programme now closely encompasses Elgianto stock. Aldonza Kennels, established for 35 years, is owned by Fay Tucker. Fay has one of the most successful kennels in Australia and Aldonza's record for Royal Show results around Australia is an enviable one. Aus. Ch. Aldonza Kistas Kid has been the most prominent sire in Australia over the last six years.

Kalina, established for more than 40 years, is the oldest active Samoyed Kennels not only in Australia but, it is believed, in the world; it is owned by Yvonne Sydenham-Clarke. Kalina must be the largest importer and breeder of

Aust. Ch. Novaskaya Royal Blaze (Imp. UK).

litters of Samoyeds in Australia. The history of the breed in Australia owes a great deal to Yvonne Sydenham-Clarke and her late husband John, for they were responsible for importing some of the stronger English lines that have given strength to the breed here today. Fairvilla Tsarovitch (Imp. UK), Eng. Aus. Ch. Imperial Rebel Of Kobe (Imp. UK) and Eng. Aus. Ch. Darryl Of Tamitsa (Imp. UK) are some of the Samoyeds imported by Mrs Sydenham-Clarke. Eng. Aus. Ch. Imperial Rebel Of Kobe (Imp. UK) can be attributed with having the largest influence on the breed today.

In New South Wales, Ray Dean's Snovink Kennel has been extremely successful. One of his top winning dogs is Aus. Grand Ch. Amundsen Hot Pursuit. This Kennel is active in obedience and agility also. The Dawnsnow Kennels have produced generations of winning stock and campaigned two Australian Grand Champions. Jo Barker of the Marydell Kennel is no longer active but she was chiefly known for her charity work undertaken with the Samoyeds, collecting thousands of dollars for the Guide Dog association. Over the years there have been many small New South Wales kennels who have had success and produced Champion stock – Arcticlight, Adeina, Rabortic, Keftin, Icemist to name but a few. Mary Fairley from Scionistir imported two Novaskaya males, Nicolai Lafay and Royal Blaze. The later was co-owned with Julie Oates.

Queensland, while a much hotter area, does have a few long-standing breeders such as Dalrod, Samdreena, Snowbay and Sunmist. Apparently Samoyeds do adjust to the warmer climate and grow coats almost as good as those in cooler areas.

In South Australia, Kossov Kennels has been successfully breeding for several years. Ellie Maitland of Kimchatka Kennels moved to South Australia from New Zealand and as her kennel partner has stayed in New Zealand, they have the best of both worlds. Kyandi and Vargo Kennels have been in existence many years.

THE SAMOYED IN AUSTRALIA TODAY

Over the years Canadian, American, European and English judges have all been delighted and surprised with the quality of the dogs they see here in Australia and the comment has been made more than once that they could compete and win at an international level. Australia is most fortunate in that because of our isolation we remain rabies-free. Most reputable breeders will only breed if the dog and bitch to be mated have both been X-rayed and hip-scored. There is not a high incidence of other disorders specific to our breed; basically Samoyeds enjoy good health. The Internet is accessible to most people to put us in immediate touch with the rest of the world for exchange of ideas, and computers also make it very easy to record pedigrees. As Neilma Fraser, New Zealand Judge and Samoyed Specialist, said after judging a specialty Show in Sydney, Australia a few years ago, "The Samoyed in Australia is in good hands!"

DENMARK

Borge Madsen, Kennel Snemark, was the first to register a Samoyed in Denmark. In 1950, he imported three Samoyeds. Two were from the UK, Snowland Nicholas from Mrs Westcott and Jewel Of The Arctic from W. Richards. The third he imported from Norway – Ibur Sheila, who was purchased from Kaare Pederson. This bitch was eventually exported to Finland and today, both in Finland and Sweden, lines are based on stock from this kennel.

In 1959, Otto Hoffman Broning decided to import, since there was only one elderly bitch left at Kennel Snemark. Again from Kaare Pederson's Kennel Ibur in Norway, he imported a bitch, Dk. Ch. Ibur Kifak. She was bred to Nord. Ch. Ibur Cinso and produced eight puppies. Otto kept one bitch, and used the kennel name Oldhojgaards. He called the bitch Oldhojgaards Sawa. In 1965, he further imported, from Sweden, Tundran's Zimba. These Samoyeds were all to become his foundation. Five litters were eventually bred.

Two of the puppies, Oldhojgaards Tanja and Oldhojgaards Balto, were sold to Kristine Steckhahn, who used them as foundation stock for her own Kennel Sammie, one of the larger and possibly most important Samoyed Kennels in Danish history. A further large Danish Samoyed kennel was established in 1966. Jyette Olsen, Kennel Jenisej, imported a bitch, Ibur Rubi, from Norway. She was mated to Tundran's Zimba. Only a few lines from this kennel are today used in breeding. From the Kennel Sammie, Inge Kisbye founded her own Kennel Antorca. She also proved to be an influential and active breeder until 1993.

The most important kennel, however, during the 1980s and early 1990s was the Kennel Kalssa of Kirsten Jorgensen.

She obtained her stock from Kennel Sammie; in particular a bitch Dk. Ch. Sammies Kaissa Petrowa. In 1983 Kirsten imported a three-year-old male from Mardee Ward in the USA. He was Int. DK Ch. Sir Jonah Of Banff, known as Sunny, and a grandson of Ch. Kiskas Karaholme Cherokee. Kennel Kaissa was to produce many top winning dogs throughout the years, and Sunny became the most used dog in Danish history, siring over 150 puppies. Almost all pedigrees of Danish Samoyeds include Sunny.

In 1985, his first litter with Sammies Kaissa Petrowa produced Multi Ch. Kaissas First Son Of Jonah. The bitch Sammies Kaissa Petrowa was herself to have enormous influence on the breed in Denmark. Although she only produced 14 puppies in three litters, most of them were used in breeding programmes. Other bitches of influence at this time were DK Ch. Kaissa's A Nuska Baltona who had six litters and 31 puppies, whilst Kaissa's Beaujolais Nouveau also produced six litters.

Samovar Charka Of Kharesi, known as Ivan, imported from Ireland, also became a well-known sire. He passed away in 1994. DK LP Ch. Kaissas Balalaika Boy Jnr. was also successfully used many times. This dog had healthy hips and became the only Danish Obedience Champion. In 1998, the best male Samoyed in Denmark was Multi Ch. Gino Of Apollon (Kaissas Leto Apollon ex Cabaka's Anais Of Ice Prince). He was bred by Gitte Morrell and owned and shown by Birgit Danielson. He went BIS at the Bundessieger in Germany. There are approximately 25 registered kennels in Denmark today.

Humoresque Jet Yacuzzi.

FINLAND

The first Samoyed to be imported to Finland was a bitch called Ibur Sheila, imported from Norway in 1952 by a blacksmith called Veikko Hofman (prefix Pajamiehen, later on Ahkion). Ibur Sheila had been mated in Denmark with Snowland Nicholas and in September 1952 she produced the first Samoyed litter in Finland. The pedigree of almost every present-day Samoyed in Finland can be traced back to these two.

In 1966 The Samoyed Association of Finland was established, being approved as the official Breed Club by the Finnish Kennel Club in 1968. Members receive four issues of their bulletin per year. There are winter and summer events and regional Clubs host sledding and training activities for Samoyed owners.

Tuula Hamalainen of Kennel Humoresque is one of the most successful breeders in Finland. Currently she is curtailing her outstanding showing career to take in her judging appointments. It was in 1982 that Tuula obtained her foundation bitch, Explorer's Wonderful Star from Birgit Hillerby in Sweden. This bitch really lived up to her name by becoming a BIS winner at Championship level and becoming a Finnish, Swedish, Norwegian, Danish Int. Champion and World Winner in Copenhagen in 1989. She was Top Samoyed in Finland in 1984, 1985, 1986 and 1989. When mated she produced 11 Champions.

Following the first Humoresque litter in 1986, four subsequent Champions went on to achieve BOB at the annual Specialty show. In 1988 Ch. Humoresque Bossanova-Boy, sired by Eng. import Sameida Springstar White Blaze ex Explorer's Wonderful Star, went on to become Top Samoyed in Finland.

American import Polarmist Mr Margeaux was also the sire of two other Humoresque Champions. In 1993, 1995 and 1997 Ch. Humoresque Quite Easy was top Samoyed. A grandson of Explorer's Wonderful Star, he had a great showing career, also becoming Finnish, Swedish, Norwegian and Int. Champion and Finnish Winner in 1995 and 1998. Finnish Winner is the title given to the BOB Winner at the main show in Helsinki. The last UK import is Roybridge Snow Dancer, sired by Eng. Ch. Zamouski Lucky Casanova At Roybridge.

GERMANY
By Annemarie Kolke
In Germany, there is no special club for Samoyeds. The Deutscher Club für Nordische Hunde (DCNH) combines Samoyeds with other sledge, herding, Nordic hunting and Asian Spitz breeds of dogs. This club has around 2,500 members and is recognised by the German Kennel CLub. The FCI Samoyed Breed Standard is the accepted breed standard in Germany. The only difference from the English Standard is that the FCI requires a Samoyed dog's height at withers to be 57cm and a bitch 53cm, with a 3cm tolerance each way. This means that Samoyeds in all FCI member countries do not only look big, they do stand higher on their legs.

Germany has twelve International Championship Shows for all FCI recognised breeds. The Deutscher Club für Nordische Hunde have five or six shows. Samoyed entries at both shows tend to be low and are dependent on foreign exhibitors. German owners of Samoyeds like to work their smiling white beauties, usually by sledding or agility, and for Germans this is much more fun than grooming and training for shows. Often the highest wins go to foreign Samoyed exhibitors, which is a pity because if the local Samoyeds were better presented, they could become more of a challenge. As it is, however, the breed is well liked and appreciated in Germany. In Germany, if a Samoyed of unknown descent is found to fit the Standard, it will be registered and under certain rules and regulations it is allowed to be bred from and given a FCI/VDH pedigree for the offspring when three fully recognised generations are known.

HOLLAND
From Eris Koops and Paul Kabel
In 1921, the first Samoyed to arrive in Holland was exported from Norway. This was Zanka Av Ostjak. He was a

grandson of the famous Sam but never bred from. In 1924, Miss Nelly Dickhoff imported three young Samoyeds from the Farningham Kennels of Mrs Kilburn-Scott. The dog, Farningham Ikon, born on February 19th 1924, and the bitch Farningham Mooswa, born on December 1st 1923, were grandchildren of Ch. Siberian Keeno; and Farningham Ural born July 3rd 1924, was a daughter of his.

Shortly after this, Miss B.A. Kuipers joined Miss Nelly Dickhoff and she eventually introduced the Samoyed to Holland as a show dog. On May 25th 1926, the first litter was born to Ikon and Mooswa. This was to become the start of the Samoya Kennel. On July 18th 1926 a second litter was born from Ikon and Ural at Kennel Duinrand. In 1929 the first Samoyed to be registered in the Dutch Stud Book (NHSB) was Farningham Mooswa of Samoya.

From 1924 to 1933, 9 dogs and 11 bitches were imported. These form the basis of Dutch breeding programmes. At the same time 253 puppies were born in the Netherlands. On August 13th 1932, the Nederlandse Samojeden Club (Dutch Samoyed Club) was officially founded by Miss Nelly Dickhoff, Mrs Van Ogten-Schoehuizen, Miss Bea Kuipers and Mr Jan Spaapen.

Between 1934 and 1937 only five dogs and two bitches were imported. After 1937, all imports stopped, the Dutch Samoyed Club advising members not to use imported dogs from England. This was because the Dutch felt that they wished to reserve the 'original type' in order to keep the breed pure. Today, these would be called working-type dogs.

There was a feeling that in the UK the type of Samoyed was altering – dogs were becoming heavier, coats longer, legs shorter and ears smaller.

HARD TIMES
During the war years from 1940-45, breeding was at a low level and during this time only 54 Samoyeds were recorded. When the Nazi leader, Hess, flew to Scotland, Miss Kuipers mated a bitch, thinking that the end of the war was near. In that litter, Samoya's Polar Queen was born. Miss Kuipers' house, near Soesterberg aerodrome, was burned down after bombing in 1944 with all the stores for her Samoyeds. Luckily, there were no casualties, but the dogs had to be evacuated.

The reduction in number of the breed had the most serious repercussions in the years after the war. Between 1950 and 1960, the numbers had so decreased that in 1957 no puppies at all were born. The period from 1945-1960 was known as the 're-building time'. Life was expensive and wages were so meagre that dogs had to take a low priority. Any puppies born had to stay with their breeder for several months because no buyers could be found. Even so, some dogs were imported that would become very important in the breeding programme.

A dog, Rippleby Davy, was imported by Wim Clay from the UK, and Selina Burema imported two bitches, Pajamiehen Beatrix and Pajamiehen Natasha, from Finland. HRH Princess Wilhelmina imported the bitch Ibur Stella, out of Snowland Stock, from Norway. She bred under her affix, Van het Aardhuis. In 1958, all these produced litters and the number of Samoyeds started to rise again. In 1960, a bitch, Anka Vom Eismer, was imported from Germany. All these names appear in the pedigree of 'original type' Dutch Samoyeds. In 1967, Miss Kuipers was admitted to hospital and a home was required for her Samoyeds. The Kabel family then took them over, becoming partners of Miss Kuipers.

BETTER TIMES

J.P. Kabel Snr. and his sons Paul Jnr. and Jan were to become important breeders, along with Martin and Sonja Hozeman, Kennel Stranja-Severna. They, and several other members of the Dutch Samoyed Club, some of whom had family ties in the UK, imported dogs from Sworddale, Lealsam, Crensa and Snowcryst Kennels. These dogs were different from the Dutch dogs and were therefore called 'English Samoyeds'. This was the beginning of a rupture in the Club. Lovers of this type of Samoyed claimed that England was the country of origin of the Samoyed breed, so the English Samoyed Standard was the right one. They argued that there had never been an 'original' Samoyed and that the

Dutch Ch. Samoya's Jingles.

Dutch breeding was one-sided back to the Farningham Kennel. This inbreeding meant that Dutch dogs developed lack of bone, big ears and short coats.

In the seventies, more dogs were imported, not only from the UK but from the USA, Canada, Sweden and Denmark. With gathering prosperity, the demand for purebred dogs grew, the number of puppies rising by 200-300 a year. Learning from the Americans, a small group started sled dog training with Samoyeds and carts on the beach at Noordwijk. It was thought that although it was well known that Samoyeds were not always successful sled dogs on polar expeditions, it was a good way to test the working spirit of the dogs. Mushers with all-Samoyed teams now sometimes even beat the Siberian husky teams.

TODAY

The majority of today's Samoyeds in the Netherlands are a middle-of-the-road mix of English, Dutch, American and Scandinavian dogs. Extreme show dogs, as shown at Crufts, are not often seen. The majority of people still believe that the truth is not always in the middle, and that old photographs and descriptions show a type of dog that deserves to be preserved, because what nature took ten to twenty thousand years to form should not be changed by men in eighty years. Others say people are changing due to better living conditions and it is no wonder that dogs change too.

One of the most prominent winning dogs in the 1990s was Dutch Ch. Samoya's Jingles (Lucky Star Jingles ex Ch. Samoya's Gloria) and grandson of Ch. Zamoyski Lucky Star Of Ostyak. Top Winning Samoyed Bitch in Holland in 1998 was Burco Leader's Dutch Lux.

Dutch Lux. Ch. Devil In Disguise.

Ch. Devil In Disguise At Snowcoat (Am. Ch. Karly Joint Venture ex Linishki Allegro).

In order to gain a title in Holland, a dog needs to obtain four CAC (Champion Certificates). A dog can enter only one class. In classes, other than puppy, the dog will get a qualification from the Judge:
U: (uitmunted) excellent
ZG: (zeer goed) very good
G: (goer) good
M: (matig) moderate
From dogs graded U, the Judge decides Best of Sex. Champions from a Breed Show receive two CAC and the reserve one CAC.

INDIA
In 1960 Eng. Ch. Snowking Of Carwood was chosen by the Indian Kennel Club to represent the standard of the Breed in India and the Asian Continent. Rex, as he was known, was Top Samoyed 1957, 1960, 1962 and 1963, when he finally retired.

IRELAND
The Irish Samoyed Dog Club was formed in 1973. Jimmy Hyland, the current Secretary, was instrumental in getting the Club started. Previous to this, there were no classes for Samoyeds at any of the Championship Shows in Ireland. The first dogs to become Irish Champions were: Arrakova Of St Nicholascript, Akim Of Snowscape, Fairvilla White Opal, Demitre Of Snowscape and Kristina Of Snowscape. The breed Championship show is held in the Glen of Imaal, Co. Wicklow. This is a beautiful spot in the middle of the Wicklow mountains, and Jimmy thinks that because of this the show is more like a garden fete. The Club has strong representation from its Irish members and every year exhibitors travel over from England, Scotland and Wales.

A group of Samoyeds at a show in Ireland.

ITALY

Among the first Samoyeds exported from England to Italy was Polar, born on January 28th 1929 from Ch. Kara Sea and Nooya. Others followed sporadically. Between 1970 and 1975, 33 puppies were born in Italy, then the breed rapidly increased. 1435 puppies were recorded in 1993. Registrations fluctuated and in 1997 only 798 were recorded. Italian breeders preferred to import stock from English lines with a few imports from the USA.

There are two Samoyed Clubs in Italy. CIRN, or the Italian Club of Northern Races, and GISS, or the Group Italian Specialist Samoyed. For the last twelve years, GISS have tried very hard to educate people about the breed in Italy through Technical Meetings, Seminars, Conferences and their magazine *Il Samoiedo*. In March 1977, an International Meeting was organised and participants attended from six European countries – Finland, Sweden, Holland, Spain, Denmark and Italy. Mrs Lesley Morgan was the representative from England. The Clan's Kennel of Eccheli Sergio is one of the oldest established ones and still very much in existence. Lines used by this kennel include Delmonte, Sworddale, Fairvilla and Kentene. In recent years, many dogs were imported from the Karazoe Kennel in England. The Polar Legend Kennel of Rivi and Finoechi produced several Champions.

Karazoe Snow Legend was imported as a puppy and became the top winning Samoyed in Italy and also in Europe. In 1994, this dog won the prestigious title Top of the Top, i.e. among all breeds that year he won the most. In recent years, other English lines have been added to Italian stock namely Novaskaya, Samont, Snowmyth, Smiliesam and Zamoyski.

Dog shows in Italy are widely spread. In order to win an Italian Championship it is necessary to win six CAC. Of these, two must be at National Shows, two at International Shows and two in Special

Bamby The Bandit At Corno Bianco.

Shows or at a Technical Meeting. In 1989, GISS organised research to be undertaken on Hip Dysplasia through a network of vets throughout the country.

NEW ZEALAND

C.E. Borchgrevinck's book, *First on the Antarctic Continent*, tells of the ship, the *Southern Cross,* landing sledge dogs on Native Island, near Stewart Island. The dogs should have been destroyed because of quarantine regulations, but permission was obtained from the New Zealand Government for them to stay. In 1901 Sir Joseph Ward, later to become Prime Minister, was given two Samoyeds by Captain Robert Scott. In 1902, the first Samoyed affix, Esquimaux, was registered by Sir Joseph. Some of the other dogs were bred from and registered with the New Zealand Kennel Club and later, during the years 1907-1909, nine others were collected and taken on Shackleton's expedition.

Captain Robert Scott also obtained 20 dogs from Samoyed tribes in Northern Siberia. In his book, *The Voyage of Discovery*, he mentions one of the bitches having a litter of four puppies. Capt. Scott gave three females and two males to the Wellington Zoo. In 1911, the Zoo imported further Samoyeds from Denmark and England. Some puppies were bred and sold to the public. None was registered with the New Zealand Kennel Club. In 1941 this Zoo section closed. Captain Scott was later given three Samoyeds by the Kilburn-Scotts for the British Antarctic Expedition of 1910-1913. Several puppies they produced were given away to Captain Scott's friends in Christchurch. One of these bitches was Nova, the other was Lady Scott.

EARLY SHOWING DAYS

The English Standard was initially adopted in 1909, with a second later adopted in 1920. In 1915, a mating between the two expedition dogs, Coona and Nova, produced Doctor, who was bred by Mr R. Thornton. Challenge Certificates were granted in 1919, firstly to the Dunedin Show, and Doctor became the first New Zealand Champion. Mr Les Burt was to make up the next Samoyed Champion in 1929. His father, a Salvation Army Officer, had been given Lady Scott. She was mated to a dog who came from a Canadian ship. The mating produced the second Champion, Prince Aututaki.

Mr Fred Zaffer became one of the pioneers of the breed. He imported Snow Chief and Snow Queen from Australia in 1932, and he became the breeder of the first Samoyed bitch Champion, White Princess Of The Yukon, who was also first to win a Group. In the 1930s, Mrs R. McNiven founded the Arctic (New Zealand) Kennels. Foundation stock was Arctic Snow, a pet dog, and Polar Aviatrix, bred by Les Burt. Numerous litters were bred and today many New Zealand Samoyeds can be directly linked to this line. Ch. Ruski Of Tsilma, with 12 BIS wins, is just one of them.

Dogs from the Pearlonna kennels of Fran and Noel Wilson can also be traced back. The Wilsons later owned one of the top producing bitches, in Ch. Pandora Of Rydal Mount. From her came nine Champions. The Yurak Kennels of Mr Dunn were yet another breeding force in the 1930s. Two Yurak Champions, Ch. Boris and Ch. Silver Knight, were bought by Mr and Mrs Williams from the Loga Kennel. In 1938 Mr and Mrs Woodhouse, Kennel Aurora, imported

Eng. NZ Ch. Rex Of The Arctic from the UK. He became the first Samoyed to win a Best in Show award. He was to collect two others.

The next Samoyed to achieve a Best in Show win was Ch. Viking Thor in 1949. That year, Mrs McNiven's niece took over the reins of the Arctic Kennel, continuing to breed, and she exported to Canada and the United States.

FROM THE FIFTIES ONWARDS

In 1955 Kay O'Connor, of the Ngaruawaha kennel, began breeding dual-purpose dogs for both obedience and showing. Her first Samoyed was Ch. Princess Kolana Of Warnick CDX. One of her subsequent dogs, Ch. Tarna, went on to win 100 Challenge Certificates. Meanwhile, in Australia, what was to be the world renowned Kalina Kennels of Yvonne Sydenham-Clarke was just becoming established. Their imported dogs and subsequent progeny were to have enormous influence in New Zealand. Major early important stud dogs were: Eng. Aus. Ch. Darryl Of Tamitsa, Aus. Ch. Starya Of Kobe and Eng. Aus. Ch. Imperial Rebel Of Kobe. A UK imported bitch Ch. Icemist Beauty was also to play a major role.

The Voinaika Kennels of Neilma and Norman Fraser began breeding in the late 1950s. Neilma is now an All Breeds Judge. Many Kalina dogs were imported by this kennel. One of the most important was (Aust. Imp) Ch. Kalina Smirnoff, a son of the famous Eng. Aus. Ch. Darryl Of Tamitsa and grandson of Aus. Ch. Icemist Beauty. With that kind of lineage, it was no wonder that he went on to produce 14 Champions.

Many excellent kennels were to emerge during the sixties – Middlemarch, Kyle, Kuhleman, Siber, Foxworth, Skrownek, Kiev and Samways. In 1961 Ch. Kalina Wanderer had a first BIS win and went on to many more. It would be 1992 before a New Zealand-bred Samoyed went BIS. This was Ch. Kuts Boy Of Chienne D'Or. 1965 saw Val and Bill Auckram's bitch, Ch. Trezor Of Belya Sobaka go BIS, being the very first Samoyed bitch to do so. Val was a co-author of *The Samoyed (New Zealand)*.

In 1966, Anne and Ross Rushbridge's Ch. Ruski Of Tsilma amassed his 12 All Breeds BIS – a record. Sandra Stewart of the Skrownek Kennel is today one of the most foremost authorities on the breed in New Zealand.

The late 1970s saw the importation of Novaskaya Stock from the UK which was to enhance a number of bloodlines, the Kimchatka Kennel of Eli Maitland and Glenys Grey being just one of these. One of the later Novaskaya imports by this prestigious kennel was NZ Ch. Novaskaya Silva Sabya, who was to become a New Zealand Top Brood

NZ Ch. Kokoda Arctic Whisper.

Bitch, producing 12 Champions.

In 1975 one of New Zealand's Top Stud dogs was born. He became NZ Ch. Snowranger Smyelchak (Ch. Kalina Silver Knight ex Malo Zneska Of Orah). He had a marvellous show career, with several Group and BIS awards. The same year, Sharon Stacey's Ch. Tarnova Imperial Yukon (Imp. Aust) was also born. He became another top New Zealand winner, with numerous BIS, six BISS and 36 Groups, including one Group win under Hans Lehtinen of Finland. He sired 15 Champions.

The Samways Kennel of Sharon Stacey and Sharon McKandry has gone from strength to strength with numerous home-bred and imported Champions. In 1981, the Samivahn Kennel of John and Paddy Watts became established in Wellington. Their foundation bitch, Ch. Snowranger Wonita, herself produced 10 Champions and they now have an amazing record with over 20 home-bred Champions to their credit. Born in 1984, and sired by the Blewitts' own top-

NZ Grand Ch. Nikolaevsk An Bye Lay.

winning Ch. Kimchatka Alexei ex Ch. Novaskaya Silva Sabya, came a grand dog: he was to become Aus. Ch. NZ Grand Ch. Kimchatka The Godfather. He has sired over 11 Champions and is the only New Zealand dog to be both an Aus. and NZ Champion. He is the most titled dog in New Zealand.

Gary and Lynn Carleton of the Zamora Kennels were to become the owners of the Top Winning Dog, NZ Grand Ch. Samways Summer Knight, known as Polar. He has notched up over 11 BIS Wins and 160 Challenges, and became The Samoyed Club's Best Samoyed Dog for a number of years. One of his progeny is Ch. Zaminka Icewalker. One of the Top Winning Bitches of 1998 was NZ Ch. Kokoda Arctic Whisper, known as Sheba, bred by Madeleine Alexander and owned by G. and P. Turner of Tauranga. She has collected 81 Challenges and a number of Speciality Wins.

Before leaving this section, the current Kennels of Kalisa, Nikolaevsk, Shoby, Sunshine and Murmansk must not go unmentioned. Also Lauren V. de C. James's Ch. Aram Khachaturian, a multi show winner and sire to both Australian and New Zealand Champions.

OBEDIENCE
Well over 20 Samoyeds have won their obedience titles in New Zealand. Amazingly, Betty Gilbert of the Siber Kennels has been training Samoyeds in Obedience and Agility for over a quarter of a century.

THE MAKING OF A CHAMPION
In the early days, the requirement was three Challenge Certificates under three different judges. Nowadays, eight CCs

under five different judges are required. A Grand Champion needs to win 50 CCs and Best in Show awards under three different judges. Although the official English Standard was adopted in 1909, a second Standard was adopted in 1920. This was revised and adopted again in 1967 to remain in line with the English Standard revised. Although the English one was revised again, New Zealand retained the 1967 version.

NORWAY

By Morten Holland and Bjorn Julseth
There were very few Samoyed dogs in Norway during the early part of the 20th Century. The few dogs that existed were either descendants of dogs used on polar expeditions or dogs which the Norwegian Lapps had obtained from the Russian Lapps. These Russian dogs were traced back to the Samoyed people of Northern Russia.

After the Second World War, although the breed existed in Norway, the standard was weak. In 1946 Kaare Pedersen started his Ibur Kennel with a bitch called Dinka and other imports he obtained from the Snowland Kennel in the UK. He also imported two dogs from the USA. Using these dogs, he was able to raise the quality of the breed in Norway to a very high standard. He was allowed to use the words "by appointment to the Queen" after he exported a Samoyed bitch, by the name of Ibur Stella (Ibur Bamsefor ex Ibur Alva), to Queen Wilhelmina of the Netherlands. In 1956, for his efforts in raising the standard of the breed in Norway, Kaare Pedersen was awarded the Norwegian Kennel Club (NKK) Silver Pin of Worthy Breed. Indeed an honour!

May Karin Borstad was also considered to feature importantly with her Maikens Kennel. She imported, from Bunty Ross in the UK, Silver Teddy Of Sworddale.

Sled dogs from the Little Rocky kennel, owned by Morten Holland and Kristen Norve.

Kaare Perdersen with the first litter of Samoyeds he bred in 1947 (Snowland Leo – Dinka).

He became a Norwegian Champion and was extensively used at stud in Norway. In recent times, a whole new generation of Samoyed breeders have stamped their characteristics on line breeding. Among those who must be mentioned are Mr and Mrs Mjaerum of the Mjaerumhogdas Kennel, Mr and Mrs Nystrand of the Finstad Kennel, Mr and Mrs Gyth of the Etahs Kennel and Astrid Klevmoen of the Buabergs Kennel. All these breeders, especially the Finstad and Etahs Kennels, have basically bred working and sled dogs. Amongst the dogs recently imported and worthy of note are Kajasac Americ Polar Bear, Nojaskaia Silva Starman, Sameida Conquest and Abakan Komolunga. Other famous Norwegian dogs are Nord. Ch. Ibur Mikko, Norwegian Ch. Bonso and Norwegian Swedish Ch. Scott.

Since there have been only a modest number of imports, the Norwegian Samoyeds on the whole are still of a similar size and weight to the old White Bjelkie, which is so like the Nansen dogs. Breeding today emphasises health, working quality, temperament and appearance. The Standard height in Norway for dogs is 57cm +/- 3cm, and for bitches 53 cm +/- 3cm. A moderate coat in terms of thickness and length is required, with the Samoyed standing rectangular and well-angled. Heavy coats and black muzzles are not considered a first priority in Norwegian breeding, and within the Standard more stress is put upon working ability. Total Samoyeds registered in Norway are approximately 1,600. Somewhere between 130 and 150 are registered annually.

The Norwegian Polar Dog Association (Norsk Polarhundklubb) includes Samoyeds as well as other Polar breeds such as the Alaskan Malamute and the Greenland dog. In Norway, the Samoyed is regarded as an excellent dog for people who enjoy outdoor activities. Sledding/Working and Showing are the main pursuits and the Samoyed is highly regarded as a happy, healthy and hard-working breed.

SPAIN
With acknowledgement to Carmen Navarro
The official Club of the Samoyed in Spain is the CEPN (Spanish Club of Nordic Dogs and Akita Inu). The first Samoyeds appeared in Spain during the late 1940s, although there is one single registration recorded in 1939. However, it is probably true to say that the first Samoyeds to influence the breed started to appear in the 1970s and were mainly from Mrs Bunty Ross's famous Sworddale Kennel in England and also some from Finland.

Toward the end of the 1980s, the breed really started to take off and become appreciated in Spain. One of the most influential dogs of that time, imported by Antonio V. Choya from Italy, was Ch. Clan's Banko (Ch. Novaskaya Georgia Prince of Astutus ex Ch. Clan's Elis). He became an International Champion, siring many Champions. Yet another important dog was EE. UU. Ch. El Al's Elegant Prince Charly (Ch. Rexann Ronderful Mr Kannuq ex Ch. El Al's Tennessee Waltz). Offspring from both these dogs has had a great influence on the breed in Spain.

The 1990s saw an even bigger escalation, with dogs again being imported mainly from England, Finland, Italy and Europe. Two dogs imported to Italy from Mr and Mrs Sharp in England were Ch. Karazoe Snow Fox and Ch. Karazoe Snow Legend. Both were to be used extensively at stud. The first was to become Mundo Int. Ita. Belg. Ch. Karazoe Snow Fox and was to take Best in Show at the Bundessieger in 1991. Antonio Choya produced some twenty Champions from his Skardu Kennel; notably, Ch. Skardu's Iberian Bear went Best in Show at Monografica de Perros Nordico's in 1995.

One of the most influential dogs to be home-bred in Spain is Esp. Int. Port. Ch. Bogart De Villaodon, Multi BIS and BISS and a son of Ch. El Al's Elegant Prince Charly. He has sired many Champions in Spain and other Villaodon Champions are to be found in Peru and Venezuela. Sp. Ch. De Villaodon Duque Of York is yet another multiple Specialty winner, his sire being Ch. Karazoe Snow Fox. Recently, many more exciting lines have been imported into Spain adding vigour and resulting in many more Champions. Notably, these include Sp. Port. Ch. Polarmist Arctic Dreams (from the USA), Am. Sp. Ch. In The Wink Of The Knight (from the USA), Am. Ch. Polar Mist Move 'N Shaker (USA), and Sp. Ch. Zamoyski Lucky Valentino, imported from the UK by the Irkuksen Kennel of Mario Babio. Annecy dogs were imported from the UK by the El Galeon Kennel. The 1998 CEPN Annual Points system winners are Ch. Polar Mist Arctic Dreams (D) owned by the De Villaodon Kennel and Ch. Villaodon Ticket (B) owned by the Nensti Kennel.

Multi BIS BISS Ch. Oso Bianco de Villaodon.

*Plogen's Anais
Sensation.*

SWEDEN

The first Samoyed was registered by the Swedish Kennel Club in 1893. On December 12th 1908 a Swedish Samoyed Standard was accepted (since revised).

By Marion Wide

Prior to the 1970s the quality of Samoyeds in Sweden was rather poor. Birgit Hillerby then developed an interest in the breed and, from the Bralandet Kennel, bought a bitch who was a daughter of the UK import Ch. Sleighprince Of Crensa. Subsequently, in 1974, Birgit imported Ch. Kayjas Cochise Of Snowcliffe from the USA. This dog was of correct size and sound temperament. Thus began Birgit's career as a breeder of Explorer's Samoyeds. Cochise was to introduce a completely new blood strain into Scandinavia. He sired 160 litters, among which were 26 Champions.

During the 1980s a Cochise grandson, Explorer's Victorio was very successful in the show ring. Meanwhile, another useful dog came into Sweden from Norway. He was Ch. Scott, born in 1982. He sired 52 puppies, many of which became sled dogs. The real recordbreaker, however, was a Cochise daughter, Explorer's Ice Star. In 1987 she was included among the Top Ten most successful dogs of all breeds in Sweden. She ranked number six and was the only bitch among that Top Ten when she was eleven years old.

In 1988, two further dogs were imported from the UK. They were Ch. Golway Adventure and Ch. Karazoe Snow Trapper. Both had the same father, Nikara Special Edition. Together, these two became influential sires, siring 256 puppies. Another successful male in the show ring at this time was Lucky Sam's Manny. The most successful dogs during the 1990s were Explorer's Moonlight

Shadow, a son of Golway Adventurer, and Elliance Escape Eagle, a grandson of Karazoe Snow Trapper. Among the bitches, Plogen's Anais Sensation was the most successful.

Top Samoyed for 1998 was Plogen's Finnish import Humoresque Stromboli, his pedigree reaching back to Cochise. Also successful in 1998 was the bitch, Swedsam's Night Flight To Venus. She was a bitch also highly qualified in Obedience.

By Annica Uppstrom
In 1996 the Svenska Polarhundklubben (Swedish Polardog Association) organised an educational conference, and one of the most important messages to come from the conference was the concept that any Samoyed show ring winner should also have the ability to take an owner home in a snowstorm. The Club's mission is to preserve the Samoyed as a working dog. Members are very mindful of the explorers Scott and Amundsen. The cold climate, with much snow in the winter, is ideal for skijoring and sled-mushing. Members get great fun from working their dogs and in the summer the Samoyeds are trained with a cart over the bare ground.

One of the most important observations about the working Samoyed is how different coats react in different climates. A Samoyed with a long, soft coat allows the snow to penetrate through to the skin and it is therefore not protective. Also it was found that a dog with a profuse coat would overheat when working. Every year a Speciality Show is held outdoors in the winter and includes a race. An average of 80 Samoyeds enter the show and 30 teams race. Of course each team can consist of as many as six Samoyeds.

In February 1999, a Nordic Championship was held and Samoyeds were specifically invited to enter from Norway, Denmark and Finland. Samoyeds in Sweden can now also gain the title Svensk Polarhund Champion. This was introduced in 1993 and is a working Championship consisting of six sections. Each dog has to run at least 160km, racing in the snow, in order to gain their title. Most dogs take two years to achieve this. Additionally, there is a working test where dogs have to compete in a race to gain the title PDP and a Working Certificate.

Average registrations of Samoyeds in Sweden is approximately 230 per year. 1989 hit a peak with 509 Samoyeds being registered with the Swedish Kennel Club. In Sweden it is considered very important to X-ray for Hip Dysplasia prior to breeding, and eye checks are also recommended. Clearly, this is an interesting Samoyed country and fanciers stress just how much they love and care for the breed.

ZIMBABWE
Irene Rowe of Harare was one of the first to import a Samoyed from the UK. In 1979, she imported a bitch from Samont stock, with which she also did obedience and agility. During her travels to Cape shows with this bitch, Irene was privileged to meet up with Ivy Kilburn-Morris (Scott). She too liked the bitch and invited Irene to her home. Irene found Mrs Kilburn-Morris to have a vast wealth of knowledge from their chats, and it was also a rewarding experience to look at all the momentoes and pictures.

Irene then imported Ch. Lireva's Karakov Of Caebryn from the UK and Ch. Mithrils Americ Of Caebryn from

S.A. Zim. Ch. Caebryn Silva Souvenir with Irene Rowe.

America. The later was to become a South African, Zambian and Zimbabwe Champion; in 1983 he also won the Sledge Dog Puppy of the Year award. Three litters were then bred. From the last came Ch. SA Zimbabwe Caebryn Silva Souvenir. This dog, known as Shane, was enormously successful in the show ring. He was described as a "dog in a lifetime", notching up 19 Best in Show wins, seven being under All Breed Judges, including Harry Spira from Australia and Pamela Cross-Stern. His sister, Ch. SA Zimbabwe Silva Spark O'Blue, also had a good show career.

Another successful top winning Samoyed in Zimbabwe was Mrs. Baynes's Ch. Annan Snow Imp Of Royana. Bred by Denise Edmondson of South Africa, this dog also had two Best in Shows to his credit. Zimbabwe's Samoyed Community is small. Although the summers are hot, the Sams cope well but do not have extensive coats. The lucky ones get to lounge round the swimming pool area. Unfortunately, when the bottom dropped out of the Zimbabwe dollar, the importation of many further Samoyeds was severely curtailed since the cost was prohibitive.

*A*PPENDIX

USEFUL ADDRESSES

Hairlooms is a small family business making distinctive gifts and keepsakes from Dog Hair. Tel: (802) 899 5192 Address: 169 River Road, Underhill, VT 05489 USA.

SAMOYED BREED CLUBS IN THE UNITED KINGDOM

THE BRITISH SAMOYED CLUB
SECRETARY: Mrs V. Freer.
Woodview, Lichfield Road,
Whittington, Lichfield,
Staffs. WS14 9JY.
Tel: 01543 433152
E-Mail: VAL@Woodview1.freeserve.co.uk

THE NORTHERN
SAMOYED SOCIETY
SECRETARY: Mrs. P.M.Taylor,
2, Delamere Park Way East,
Cuddington, Cheshire.
CW8 2UE.
Tel: 01606 889665
E-Mail Taylornaduska@aol.com

THE SAMOYED ASSOCIATION
SECRETARY: Mrs A. Chambers,
Boundary House,
Thrapston Road, Bythorn,
Huntingdon, Cambs. PE18 0RA.
Tel: 01832 710436

THE SAMOYED BREEDERS
& OWNERS LEAGUE
SECRETARY: Mr. J.I. Rees,
19 Richmond Crescent,
Islington, London N1 0L2.
Tel: 020 7607 8971

USA

SAMOYED CLUB OF AMERICA
CORRESPONDING SECRETARY:
Lori Elvera
3711 Brices Ford Court
Fairfax, VA 22033
Tel: (703) 476-0735
E-mail: bayousam@hotmail.com
www.org/samoyed_club_of_america.html

LOCAL SAMOYED CLUBS

ANTIETAM CREEK SAMOYED
CLUB, INC.
SECRETARY: Shannon Hurry.
LIAISON: Stacey Arcieri,
2768 Winston Ct, Woodbridge,
VA 22191
Tel: (703) 221-6683

BARBARY COAST SAMOYED CLUB
SECRETARY: Tami Lynch
LIAISON: Tami Lynch, 1066 Scott St,
Fairfield, CA. 94533-4171.
Tel: (707) 422-1909

CHICAGOLAND SAMOYED
CLUB, INC.
SECRETARY: Karen Macaluso
LIAISON: Mary A. Frederick,
2221 N. 2829th Rd, Marseilles,
IL 61341.
Tel: 815-434-4030

DENVER SAMOYED
ASSOCIATION, INC.
SECRETARY: Thalia Peletis
LIAISON: Debbie Sencenbaugh,
3811 Royal Dr, Ft Collins,
CO 80526-2943.
Tel: (970) 223-8238

DELAWARE VALLEY
SAMOYED CLUB
SECRETARY: Lori Stockert
LIAISON: Nancy Stitley,
144 Commissioners Rd,
Mullica Hill, NJ 08062.
Tel:(609) 478-6428

GREATER PITTSBURGH
SAMOYED CLUB, INC.
SECRETARY: Tracy Hunter

LIAISON: Tracy Hunter,
904 Stevendale Drive,
Pittsburgh, PA 15221.
Tel: (412)271-2013

EASTERN GREAT LAKES
SAMOYED FANCIERS
SECRETARY: Gail Pepe
LIAISON: Gail Pepe, 9971 Larkin Road,
Eden, NY 14057.
Tel: (716) 337-2350 E-
Mail:Winepro@Earthlink.net

HEART OF AMERICA
SAMOYED CLUB
SECRETARY: Lynn Scheffner
LIAISON: Cyndy Wedel,
3737 S 215th St, Goddard,
KS 67052.
Tel: 316-794-8700.
E-Mail: mcwedel.msn.com

METROPOLITAN ATLANTA
SAMOYED CLUB
SECRETARY: Cathy Pendleton
LIAISON: Cathy Pendleton,
1268 Hasty Trail, Canton,
GA 30115.
Tel:(770) 479-6800.
E-Mail: bestovbreed@mindspring.com

MICHIGAN SAMOYED RESCUE
SECRETARY/LIAISON:
Melissa Howell, 13365 Vernon Dr,
Grand Ledge, MI 48837.
Tel: (517) 627-0048.
E-Mail: Melhow@aol.com

MINUTEMAN SAMOYED CLUB
SECRETARY: Helen Sullivan
LIAISON: Peggy Gaffney,
877 Marion Rd, Cheshire, CT 06410.
Tel: (203) 272-8548

NORTHERN CALIFORNIA
SAMOYED FANCIERS
SECRETARY: Julie Osterman
LIAISON: Susan Rath-Fewlass,
8312 Wilderness Oaks Ct,
Oakdale, CA9S361-92S4.
Tel: (209) 845-2278
E-mail: snoflyte@aol.com

NORTHERN ILLINOIS
SAMOYED ASSISTANCE, INC.
SECRETARY: Jacki Shadinger
LIAISON: PO Box 218,
Arlington Heights, IL 60006
Tel: (847) 392-5000
E-Mail: mcdudelte@aol.com

POTOMAC VALLEY
SAMOYED CLUB
SECRETARY: Marge Goodenough
LIAISON: Nancy Hermle,
429 Lewis S,
NW Vienna, VA 22180.
Tel:(703) 938-1423
E-Mail: LazySam@aol.com

PRAIRIELAND SAMOYED
CLUB, INC.
SECRETARY: Dennis Hampton
LIAISON: Kent Lack,
1387 Newcastle Lane, Bartlett, IL 60103.
Tel: (630) 830-5299
E-Mail: kent.lack@antec.com

SAMOYED ASSOCIATION
OF MADISON, INC.
LIAISON: Jane Hirst
Tel: (444) 375-0737
E-Mail: dhirst@execpc.com

SAMOYED ASSOCIATION
OF METRO DETROIT
LIAISON: Jim Becklund,

1171 E Webb Rd, Dewitt, MI 48820.
Tel: (517) 669-3020
E-Mail: Xamoyedx@aol.com

SAMOYED ASSOCIATION
OF MINNEAPOLIS-ST.PAUL
SECRETARY: Kathy Mackai
LIAISON: Laura Wolfe,
2228 Byrant Ave N, Minneapolis,
MN 55412-2538
Tel: (612) 529-3930. S.A.M.S.Internet
web page: http://www.Winternet.com/-
Midnight/SAMS

SAMOYED CLUB OF AUSTIN, INC.
SECRETARY: Debbie Buid
LIAISON: Joan Auld,
3310 Catalina Drive, Austin,
TX 78741.
Tel: (512) 441-6912
E-Mail: Snovit@Texas.net

SAMOYED CLUB OF
CENTRAL ARIZONA
SECRETARY: Pam Hofmann
LIAISON: Pam Hofmann,
1014 E Carson Dr, Tempe,
AZ 85282.
Tel: (480) 838 8163
E-Mail: Jphofmann@aol.com

SAMOYED CLUB
OF HOUSTON
SECRETARY: Anne Peil
LIAISON: Pam Barbe,
16411 Graven Hill, Spring,
TX 77379.
Tel: (281) 320-0914
E-Mail: pbarbe@pdq.net

SAMOYED CLUB
OF LOS ANGELES
SECRETARY: Kathy Ward

LIAISON: Kathy Ward,
Fallbrook, CA 92028-9489.
Tel: (706) 731-2141

SAMOYED CLUB OF
WASHINGTON STATE, INC.
SECRETARY: Rene Brimhall
LIAISON: Darlene Rautio
Tel: (206) 932-5830
E-Mail: sistoo@aol.com

SAMOYED FANCIERS OF
CENTRAL FLORIDA
SECRETARY/LIAISON: Chery West,
328 Bridle Path, Casselberry,
FL 32707.
Tel: (407) 699-5329

SAMOYED RESCUE OF
SOUTH TEXAS, INC.
SECRETARY: Carol Brown,
Heather Schmidt, 1181 Catalpa Circle,
Houston, TX 77065.

SAN FRANCISCO
SAMOYED RESCUE
SECRETARY: Anna & Paul Gramlin
LIAISON: Denise Howell (President),
PO Box 6852, San Carlos,
CA 94070.
Tel: (415) 451-7175
E-Mail: Samrescue@Samoyed.org
www.samoyed.org/sfsr.html

WILLAMETTE VALLEY
SAMOYED FANCIERS
SECRETARY: Debbie Dassie
LIAISON: Kaye Sawyer,
573 NE Osborne Ct, McMinnville,
OR 97128.
Tel: (503) 472-5418
E-Mail: Mystsams@macnet.com

AUSTRALIA

THE SAMOYED CLUB
OF VICTORIA INC.
SECRETARY: Mrs Ann Pederson
PO Box 1103, Box Hill 3128.

INTERSTATE CLUBS

NSW Samoyed Club
SECRETARY: Mrs Vivenne Zavattaro,
14 Samoa Ave, Picnic Point 2213.

ACT Samoyed Club
Kylie Whitehill, PO Box 523,
Erindale Centre 2903.

SA Samoyed Club
Mrs P. Fletcher, 10 Boulevard, Tea Tree
Gully 5091.

QLD Samoyed Club
Mrs R. Ford, Silkwood Estate, 16
Bellmore Ct, Pine Mountain 4306.

DENMARK

THE SAMOYED CLUB OF
DENMARK (founded in 1980)
President: Henrik Soeborg
Hjelmsolillevej 1, 4171 Glumso,
Denmark.

FINLAND

THE SAMOYED ASSOCIATION
OF FINLAND
Secretary: Eeva Tynkkynen,
Utola, Haavistontie, Finland,
168, 37140 Nokia.
Tel: 00 358 3 342 3815
E-mail: eeva.tynkkynen@sci.fi

HOLLAND

DUTCH SAMOYED CLUB
Secretary: Corry van de Ham,
Gouidenstein, 48 3772 LD,
Barneveld, Netherland.
Tel. 00 31 342 413809

IRELAND

THE IRISH SAMOYED CLUB
Hon. Sec. James Hyland,
Davidstown, Kelshamore, Donard,
Glen of Imaal, Co. Wicklow.
Tel: 00353 4540 4766

ITALY

**GRUPPO ITALIANO
SPECIALIZZATO SAMOIEDO**
SECRETARY: Paula Daffunchio
"La Valletta", Via S Biagio, 37
27045 Casteggio (PV), Italy.
Tel/Fax: 0383 82227
E-mail: giss@geocities.com

NEW ZEALAND
**AUCKLAND PROVINCIAL
SAMOYED ASSOCIATION**
Secretary: Sharon Kelly

516 Ormiston Road, R.D.I. Manurewa,
New Zealand.

DOMINION SAMOYED CLUB
Secretary: Carol Fleming
Burnham Road East, Burnham PDC
Christchurch 8191, New Zealand.

THE SAMOYED CLUB
Secretary: Gary Carleton
State Highway 1, R.D. The Horo 6470,
New Zealand.

SWEDEN

SVENSKA SAMOJEDRINGEN
This Club has many members and
emphasises the Samoyed as an all-round
family dog. SECRETARY: Mariann Wide
Champinjonvagen 14,
756 45 Uppsala, Sweden.
E-Mail: leif.wide@klinkem.uas.luk.se

The Svenska Polarhundklubben (Swedish
Polardog Association) includes other Polar
breeds as well as Samoyeds. It is
recognised by the Swedish Kennel Club.
SECRETARY: Annica Uppstrom
Ammenas 8360
451 91 Uddevalla, Sweden.